# CREATIVE

# PROFESSIONAL

# PHOTOGRAPHY

# CREATIVE

# PROFESSIONAL

# PHOTOGRAPHY

## by Robin Perry

ZIFF-DAVIS PUBLISHING COMPANY     NEW YORK

ZIFF-DAVIS PUBLISHING COMPANY

Printed in the United States of America
Library of Congress Catalog Number 79-66281
ISBN 0-87165-031-2

First Printing

*I dedicate this book to my heirs—all the young professionals who choose photography as their life's work and as a way to earn their living, who love the art of photography and who devote their lives, their souls and their creativity to the ever-elusive quest for perfect photographs.*

# Contents

AUTHOR'S NOTE ............................................................. 11

PROLOGUE: An Endangered Species ...................... 13

## PART 1     CREATIVITY

1 No More Excuses ..................................................... 20

2 Evaluate Yourself ..................................................... 27

3 The Quality of Being Principled ......................... 31

4 Warning! Contrived Photograph ......................... 36

5 Helen and Ralph and the Kodak Color Print
     Replicator................................................................. 41

6 Knowledge, the Key to Success............................. 47

7 Books, Books and More Books............................. 53

8 The New Breed .......................................................... 60

9 Provincialism—and the Ways out of It .............. 64

10 The Photographer and the Economy .................. 69

11 Hypnosis, Transcendental Meditation and
     Other Goodies ......................................................... 74

**12** Fame and Pride ............................................... 80

**13** A Fairy Tale, Perhaps a Fable? ....................... 85

**14** The Photographer As Artist............................. 91

# PART 2 PROFESSIONALISM

**15** Marketing Your Photography ........................... 99

**16** Pricing Problems and Customs ...................... 104

**17** Protect Yourself............................................ 116

**18** Selling Your Rights ....................................... 122

**19** What's a Right, and What Isn't ....................... 128

**20** The Photographer As Publisher....................... 134

**21** Managing Your Money ................................... 140

**22** Intimidation ................................................. 146

**23** Speculative Photo-Graphic Illustration ............. 152

**24** Spatial Impressions As First Aid...................... 155

**25** The Planned Disaster .................................... 160

**26** Learn to Say No............................................ 165

**27** Time: The Critical Resource ........................... 170

**28** The Photographic Control Commission ........... 177

**29** The Modernization of the Photographer........... 182

**30** The Coloroid Dry Process Corporation ............. 188

**31** What Makes a Professional Successful ............. 194

# PART 3 TECHNIQUE

**32** Basic Camera Techniques ............................. 201

**33** Format Comparisons .................................... 207

**34** Lenses—Wide, Normal and Telephoto ............... 210

**35** Extension Tubes and Tele-Extenders ................. 215

**36** Why a Focal Plane Shutter ................................... 220

**37** The Unseen World ................................................. 224

**38** The Importance of Duping ................................. 230

**39** Metering Techniques ............................................ 233

**40** Supermeter! The Exposure Meter of the

Future ........................................................................ 238

**41** Light and Lighting ............................................... 244

**42** Light It Right ........................................................ 253

**43** Strobe Lighting Techniques ................................ 259

**44** Copying Techniques Simplified ......................... 265

**45** Redefining the Element ....................................... 270

**46** Space Perceptions ................................................ 275

**47** What You See Isn't What You Get ...................... 281

**48** Photographers' Popular Misconceptions ............ 286

EPILOGUE: Some Thoughts on the Future .......... 297

# Author's Note

This book is a collection of essays on the photographic profession. Many of the chapters were originally written for the *Dexter Bulletin,* and I am grateful for their permission to reprint. Other chapters were written in response to the needs and problems of the professional photographers attending my Creative Color Workshops. Those chapters laced with points of technique are aimed at directing newer members of the profession to the methods and equipment used in the types of creative photography that sell best.

The first section of this book contains essays designed to help the photographic practitioner to understand the medium and his or her relation to it.

11

The second section pertains to more practical aspects of photography as a profession and business. The third section is made up a series of quick references, how-to chapters and snippets of practical, technical information. There is some overlapping, since I sometimes find it helpful to bring in background from one chapter to develop a point in another. A quick reread of the relevant material just before handling a particular assignment may be quite helpful.

Nothing trains a photographer more quickly than experience. Each new experience adds to the individual's total wisdom. Trial and error is a costly methodology—too costly, considering our present economy. Photographers can no longer afford to experiment on each assignment. If a given assignment is approached with a careful technical understanding of the limitations involved along with a *creative* comprehension of how to perform well, the photographer will have a better chance of success. All assignments are actually variations of previously confronted challenges.

*Robin Perry*
*June 1979*

# Prologue: An Endangered Species

Everything I read tells me that the next endangered species is the professional photographer. Make no mistake—this is no authorial cuteness. An opinion? Yes, but give it a closer look.

Thirty million. That's 30 million *still* cameras sold in the United States last year alone! Many were of the Instamatic variety, but that's still a lot of cameras. The year before, the figure was more like 20 million—a mere bagatelle, and 20 years ago, such sales were only a million or so. How about this little series of statistics? Eastman Kodak produced 5,500,-000,000 color prints in 1978! No matter how you slice it, that's a lot of prints from one company. Would you say Kodak's production represents 50 percent of the market? Okay—let's add another 5,500,000,000 prints from all the other laboratories in the country—and that's conservative. Now we're talking about 11,000,-000,000 color prints at least and 30,000,000 still cameras—all in one year. Formidable competition for the small studio—portrait or commercial.

Now guestimate what these figures were for previous years. Through extrapolation we find that the annual increase in such activity is about 15 percent. Count that growth of previous years with the present year and next year and you come up with some mind-boggling figures that suggest enormous competition for the professional photographer. At one time, the number of successful prints from an amateur roll of negatives was three per roll of 20 and six per roll of 36. The figure today is more like 16 out of 20 and 28 out of 36—it pays to invent cameras that guarantee successful prints or transparencies. Add automatic cameras, automatic focusing and all the other available foolproof features, and you can see why there is money in the amateur photofinishing market. Successful prints and transparencies result in more and more profit for the manufacturer, the photofinishing laboratory and the photo dealer. Success breeds success: more and more cameras are sold, more and more prints are made, and more and more professional photographers fail.

When I first went into the photographic studio business in 1936, photography was the mystery of the ages. We photographers did some mumbo-jumbo under the black cloth and presto! we had a photograph. There were darn few amateurs, almost no moonlighters, and our customers knew very little of the process. Schools and colleges hired the professionals as did industry. When a family wanted a high quality portrait they went to the professional's studio or he came to the house. Industries called on the professional or specialized photographer for their work. Not so today.

Every one of those 30,000,000 cameras and many from the previous years are working hard against the professional—albeit unknowingly or unintentionally. Dad takes many of the baby pictures that used to be taken by the professional; children's portraits are taken yearly by a specialized group every year, even through college. Some teachers are now moonlighting, taking school photographs themselves and using the specialized laboratories to make up the packages. Dad goes to the office and becomes Mr. Middle Manager or Mr. Executive. He's more than conversant with photography—more important, he understands the cost structure. He can't see why someone in the company doesn't do some of the necessary photography, so he queries the plant personnel manager and finds they have at least a dozen people "interested in photography," willing to take the slides for the Annual Report. When a professional shows up with his Canon, Pentax, Minolta or what have you, the manager engages the photographer in a discussion of the relative merits of the Canon, Pentax, Minolta systems and decides his is better—whatever better is.

Finally the bill arrives and Mr. Middle Manager sees that the photographer has charged $300-$400-$500-$600 per day, or more. The executive decides his salary of $600 a *week* doesn't compare with that and wonders if he should have been a professional photographer. He suggests to management that in the future the company use him at half the professional's rate. After all, he has better equipment with the new automatic exposure control, the ASA 400 Ektachrome and the new filtration control and the new focusing control and the new powerful automatic flash control.

This scenario may seem farfetched—but is it? It seems that much of the new technology is working against the professional. In recent issues of *Photographic Marketing,* the magazine of the Photographic Marketing Association, dealers were exhorted to "get involved" with their customers by holding seminars for amateurs such as a "baby picture day" at the store. Other stores are showing and teaching how to shoot and market Little League pictures. Another store publishes a newsletter with advice on how to light for portraits and wedding photography. Some of the magazines are suggesting that readers seek help from camera stores on how to photograph cars.

The PMA has an Idea Exchange Service containing those mentioned and many more "to help promote your business." The binder is five dollars— maybe photographers should send for it.

I don't blame the PMA or the photo dealers— they're just doing their job and that's why they're members. Advice about darkroom photography, color printing and how to take pictures is part and parcel of the photo dealer's promotion of his business. More power to him. What is more important is, who is speaking for you? Where is your lobby? Are you organized? And another is, can you see the erosion and inroads into professional photography by these cameras and photofinishing laboratories?

Many of these areas that were once exclusively the professional's are now common to any owner of the new sophisticated cameras. There's got to be less earned income in the area of baby photography, portraits, wedding photography and some industrial photography in spite of the increase in the population. There are more moonlighters now than ever before and fewer studios than recorded in the 1960 census. What this means is that the professional must find areas where the amateur can't step in—opportunities that are simply unavailable to amateurs. There are such areas.

One is the large format studio catalogue and illustration. Barring a recession, there'll always be room for this type of photography. The problem here is the enormous cost of setting up or even beginning to set up such a studio. The recent reevaluations of the German mark, the Swiss franc and the Japanese yen have priced the equipment so high as to be virtually unobtainable without a massive loan. Setting up such a studio, then, is available, like politics, only to those with money. A frightening situation but a reality, nonetheless. Parallel with the need for equipment or the money for it is the requirement for some rather sophisticated knowledge of that type of photography. I recently did a series of ordinary photographs for the Heublein Company. The shots, all on 8 × 10 chromes, are deceptively simple—a glass or a bottle sitting on top of a can of liquor. I've had graduates of photographic schools look at them with contempt as "simplistic." Yet, there're far from it, as any other 8 × 10 catalogue specialist will tell you. I almost can't teach one how to do them since so much of the basic necessary knowledge is not possessed by most students. How do you build a house on a sand foundation?

The other area is in high quality 35mm color illustrations for a wide variety of clients and sold mostly by speculation to magazines, record companies, greeting card companies, poster publishers and, of all things, background for blister packagers. This type of photography needs much less equipment, no studio, no location, no employees, but a lot of creativity and a smart business head. This type is easily the best for a photographer wishing to change careers in mid-stream and is generally the type I teach in my Creative Color Workshops.

Between or parallel to these two areas are many specialized areas such as architecture, medicine and making brochures and catalogue sheets for clients, to name three disparate types. But for the vast majority of small photographers trying to make a living, the field is narrowing down—winnowing out—many of the old timers and many of the dilettantes. Darwin called this the process of Natural Selection, or the Survival of the Fittest. Whatever you call it, the professional photographer is an endangered species.

# PART 1
## Creativity

# 1 No More Excuses

I have little patience with photographers who complain about coupon or department store portrait competition. Quite obviously they're already at the bottom of the financial barrel and really shouldn't be in the photographic business at all.

There's little excuse for a photographer not being successful in this day and age—perhaps the only reason that I can think of is that he or she isn't capable either technically or mentally and isn't ever likely to change. That sort is clearly endangered. This doesn't mean one hasn't the right to be a photographer—I don't deny him that—but all the seminars, workshops and schools aren't going to give him the one ingredient no one else can give him—motivation, or ambition, if you like.

Every magazine is looking for good illustrations or some form of photography. They're forever looking for competent photographers who can develop their own themes and stories almost without assignment, and who can execute these stories without direction. This places an enormous responsibility on the photographer, far beyond the capabilities of the average studio photographer hired to take a photograph, to produce a print or transparency, to make a portrait, to copy or whatever. Such skills as these, once considered within the realm of only the professional photographer, are now considered as ordinary techniques most of which are so simple that the art director or businessman can handle them himself with today's modern automatic cameras and the proliferation of color laboratories.

Anyone can take a photograph, few can make a series, and still fewer can make a picture story that is well coordinated with text as well as illustration. I'm not suggesting that photographers become photojournalists but I am suggesting that clients need and, further, expect, more from today's photographers than they're getting. It's interesting to note that this type of photographer, the thematic or creative, is always successful regardless of the economic condition of the country and usually contrary to the financial condition of the photographic business as a whole.

Most big businesses maintain marketing departments whose main job is to determine what the consumer needs, wants, or can be programmed to need or want now or in the near future. Many of these same companies have new-product development boards to do similar research. The reason this research is done is to insure a healthy financial condition in the future. Few if any professional photographers try to see beyond the end of the next exposure.

The problem stems from the fact that photographers are in photography because they're fascinated with the craft, and early on they found that there are some people who will purchase photographs or hire a photographer to take photographs and pay good money. Beyond that most don't want to be bothered with anything connected with conducting a business. Moreover, most photographers are totally inept when it comes to business procedures. For those that have succeeded, if you scratched the surface of their background, you'd see that they were either trained or had a natural bent toward business. How often have you seen photographs taken by famous photographers and said to yourself, "Hell, I can do just as well." The point is, you didn't, you don't and you aren't the professional he or she is. Just because you have one better photograph (and who is to judge which is better?) than the published professional doesn't necessarily mean that you are as good.

One rather glaring difference is that the real professional can produce consistently. Even if you are a better photographer, you may not be a better businessman—and remember that being a businessman is part and parcel of being a *professional photographer.* Without business sense, you will never be successful. If photography is just your hobby, then for heaven's sake stop deluding yourself and earn your living doing something else. If photography is your way of earning the bread on the table, then recognize that being a business person is part of the total professional photographer.

Being a business person is still not enough to make one successful. There is also the requirement of simply being intelligent enough to be a master of many other skills. Marketing research had damn well better be one of those skills. If you can't see that photography is changing daily, weekly and monthly, and at an alarming rate, then you don't read or you're a mole. Just read the photographic magazines of five years ago and see the changes wrought in that short time span. Speculate on what some uses of photography will be in five years.

Who would have imagined five years ago that there would be a television set (Panasonic) with the technology to deliver an $8\frac{1}{2} \times 11$ color print of a still section of the commercial appearing on the set? Both 3M and Xerox have the capability of copying color art or transparencies and producing either a contact or an enlarged color print. True, the quality still isn't up to what we have come to expect, but it will be there soon. Your television set will soon become a "Home Communication Center." Probably within five years you will be able to receive video-telephone messages from the set. Sony's Betamatic recorder can duplicate the sound and color image program directly from your set. You can be watching one program while your Betamatic is recording something on another channel. Do you feel that these examples of existing technology are remote from you as a photographer? I'd suggest you contemplate the effects they could have on your profession. Let's get closer to home. Take all the squeeze tubes you've used during the past five years as an example. You've probably used toothpaste, shaving cream and perhaps suntan lotion, to name three. A trip to any supermarket or drugstore will reveal at least twenty more. I know because I tried to list all of them. Right now the technology doesn't exist to print a half-tone in color on those tubes. Oh, it can be printed on the tube, but as the tube is squeezed the print will flake off. Manufacturers are reluctant to produce half-tone tubes because of this problem and possible suits should the ink be toxic. Line-tone can be and is printed on tubes at present. Can you imagine the thousands of photographs that will be used when this technology comes about?

This is just one small example of where the photographer should do his own marketing research. I invented a series of empty white lead tubes with superimposed scenics in color to suggest freshness for the toothpaste, warmth and color for the suntan lotion and morning coolness for the shaving cream. Would you like to know what I did with them? Easy; I contacted every manufacturer of the product, not the tubes, and suggested that I was ready for the new technology and further suggested that perhaps they could use my services. Well, I have some very complimentary letters and more important, I have some jobs. I had assumed, and I was correct, that a photographer who could think ahead would be capable of offering more than their regular photographer. Anyway, the program cost little and brought my photography to the attention of some prospective clients.

The point is, color photography for packaging hasn't even scratched the surface of its potential. Clients were impressed with this "sales gimmick" of mine, as were the art directors at the agencies. Many clients and agencies think I just might come up with something innovative using *their* product.

You never show "ordinary" photography to a client or an art director. You always show novel or creative photographs so that they can see the application of your photography to their needs. Often I'll show wildly creative photography and get an ordinary assignment. This is to be expected.

Where do you get the ideas? Mostly from reading. I find the best magazine by far for a commercial photographer is *Fortune.* I read it cover to cover and scan the ads. Reading this one magazine gives me a feel of where business is now and where it is going. Most of the advertisers show off their new products, services or sometimes just ideas. I'm often able mentally to jump ahead of what I read and anticipate the next move or invention. I've been a subscriber to *Fortune* for about 20 years, and now I feel I have a touch for big business that helps me with my creative photography. Another magazine, incidentally, published by the same company is *Time.* But with *Time* I'm interested in current events rather than business. After all, some of the best journalists are writing for these two magazines. Why shouldn't I take advantage of them? I scan and I clip about 30 magazines a month. I read all of them—magazines of art, literature, the humanities and current events and business. The ideas come from all but the photographic magazines. I use the photographic magazines for news of the profession and new products.

Again I say, don't complain about competition, or the economy—these are only excuses. Branch out, drop the idea that you are tied to your locality. Expand your own knowledge, and then approach anyone, anywhere.

# 2 Evaluate Yourself

Most corporations in the United States and other Western countries conduct some sort of performance evaluation of their executives and other personnel at least once a year. The systems and how they are used are as varied as the people who conduct them, but the objectives are always the same: to determine the on-going usefulness of the employees and to identify those with greater potential than is being tapped at the time. This prevents good people from being overlooked for promotion, and it helps to stimulate workers to greater productivity.

Performance evaluation helps the company and it helps the employee, too. Similarly, in the military, "fitness reports" render valuable services all around.

27

What have these things to do with the freelance photographer? Actually, quite a lot. We photographers don't have specific and formal evaluations of our performance; no one sits down with us to tell us our faults in conducting our business. We don't receive professional advice on how to improve our ways of working. Most of the real improvement that a photographer accomplishes comes from qualities and improvements within himself or herself. His determination to improve relates directly to his income. For instance, greater patience makes for better photographs. Persistence pays off in the form of orders. Honesty develops better and more lasting relationships with customers. Improving his technique enables the photographer to enhance the quality of his product, which results in a higher income. Inquisitiveness causes him to read more and therefore to try new things. Drive—the power that gets things done, that keeps one working through fatigue, that pushes the winner past the losers—drive comes with the reflections of honest self-evaluation and is the hallmark of the upwardly mobile freelance photographer. And he develops them alone.

It takes a certain type of individual to work alone or independently, without supervision or direction. Many individuals drift into occupations where their success will be entirely dependent upon what they alone can do. These individuals sometimes think that the fateful move was made by luck or chance, when, in fact, they actually have a great ability to operate by themselves. To work alone successfully, to be a truly creative professional photographer, one must have, before anything else, self-discipline.

"Performance evaluations" discover these traits,

and wise executives promptly find tasks for such employees where initiative and independent action are plentiful—else the employees won't remain employed there long. Desperate for creative action, many people seek freelance type tasks for themselves. I suppose that if we were children in school, we *freelance* photographers would be called achievers.

The point is that it behooves us to understand ourselves, and if we work best alone using some or all of the qualities mentioned above, then so be it. To make the most of that capacity, be sure to have your own performance self-evaluations.

Our country has been turning over a new leaf. Government as well as private individuals are reevaluating themselves and their respective characters. What we once considered old-fashioned is now the new ethic. Honesty, loyalty, fair play and high principles are slowly taking on new meaning as marks of character. The energy shortage is making people more dependent upon each other. The family, which for years has been torn asunder by the headlong pace of technology and mechanization, has suddenly begun to experience a need for togetherness.

This country is going through major changes in all directions. Those of us who are freelance photographers must recognize that there is an even greater reward and a greater economy on the other side of this present situation. We have only to reevaluate our needs and take in a notch in the proverbial belt. We need but firm up our convictions about what we want to do, concentrate harder on immediate tasks, solve problems as they occur, work harder to take better pictures and to sell more of them. It may mean more hours of work, combining calls to save gas and using the telephone to firm up appointments rather than making blind calls, and using the mails for directed selling campaigns—here again to save calls.

Evaluate your performance over the last year and find your errors. List them and then correct them. Make a list of your positive abilities and another of the characteristics that get in the way of your success. It may be that New Year's resolutions are old-fashioned, but it's good to take stock of yourself from time to time.

Remember: if you have the ability to work independently, then you must be your own executive and you must answer to yourself.

Above all, your final product, the photograph, has to be as near-perfect as possible for the purpose that you have in mind. The time of making the photograph is the time that will separate the successful photographer from the failures. A *good photograph,* carefully exposed and of the highest quality, is a must. There are no excuses for poorly executed photographs.

You can learn what you don't now know. Almost every magazine runs a scillion how-to articles. Kodak puts out a booklet on some technique or problem almost every day. Good equipment helps, no question about that, but knowledge is better. Plan your business attack just as carefully. Anticipate the changes in our lifestyle, and you will be able to capitalize on them.

# 3 The Quality of Being Principled

I dislike being maudlin about the need for all of us to reevaluate our character from time to time, but the older I get, the more I subscribe to the value of being highly principled and of good moral stature. More important, I think of being principled as a business asset. This was brought to my attention recently at a luncheon with some business friends. We were discussing the "welfare ripoff," "shoplifting" and how so many people feel that if they can cheat big business, not necessarily by illegal means as much as by some form of manipulation, they have "beaten the system." Sometimes their successes are publicized and I am shocked that the media lends them support, which in my mind makes the media less principled,

31

also. Cheating, "ripping off" insurance companies, manipulating people for personal gain, taking advantage of loopholes in the law and in general supporting immoral characteristics can only result in a nation of mental degenerates.

Photographers are unique in many ways, but perhaps in the best sense they are always looking for the *best* way to portray a person or an object. They look for the most flattering light or an angle that enhances, and constantly strive to *improve* their photography. Such a positive attitude, carried on for years, can mean only a highly developed character with empathy for all of life.

Imagine the effect on a respected photographer's character of 20 years of photographing people. He or she must have developed great understanding and a feeling of real love for people, else he could not be successful. A commercial photographer, too, can only have so improved himself during the days, weeks and months of trying to make better commercial photographs. If I had to pick a *friend* by his career, I would pick a photographer.

But we're all being beset upon by the "Watergates" and the continuously disturbing news in papers, magazines and on television. This constant sensationalism and the emphasis placed on the seamy side of life is wearing away at the character of all of us. This constant chipping at the moral fibre will sooner or later cause us to rebel and across this country will come a resurgence—a ground swell of moral rebellion and, I would hope to see, a reevaluation of our moral concepts. But we should remember Adlai Stevenson's remark ". . . it is often easier to fight for principles than to live up to them. . . ."

There's a drunk in my town, quite harmless, but sometimes he wanders out into traffic where we worry about him. But the locals are patient, we don't blow our horns, mostly because we like to watch his dog. She's a big mongrel, one-third collie, one-third German shepherd and one-third anything else you can think of, and she adores her man. Instinctively she'll move out in front of him blocking a car's path; she'll rub up against him sometimes on the sidewalk to move him out of harm's way. Nobody trained her —she just knows her master needs her. She looks up at him sometimes with a look of pure worship—a look I'd give a lot to have. Sometimes he sits alongside a building getting the winter sun with his dog— I often hear him talking to her. Whatever their communion, God has blessed them with a love not many others have. I've always believed you can tell the goodness of a person by the way a child or an animal treats him or her. For some unaccountable reason, God has given the "innocents" among us an insight far beyond their years. Their instinct is usually infallible. Someday I'm going to capture on film the look of pure devotion those two have for each other. My problem is that every time I get near enough to get the photograph I want I become enveloped in the aura of their mystique and it just seems sacrilegious to poke a camera in the face of God's light.

I'm convinced that the more we help each other as photographers the more we improve ourselves. It took me years to rid myself of jealousy of other photographers and even today I suffer an occasional twinge. I can well remember those who disliked other photographers entering their studio or darkroom for fear they would lose a client or the visitor would learn their "trick." This is a character flaw. It really means they suffer from insecurity. For almost all of my photographic life I've helped anyone I can and many times at great expense to me. Don't get me wrong—I'm no goody-two-shoes, but I do believe that the more people I help, the more I gain in terms of business, or more important, in improvement in my character.

Because of this attitude of looking for the best way to photograph something or someone, photographers are usually highly principled as people and highly ethical as businesspersons and rarely do they try to cheat. Of course every trade and profession has its share of bad apples, but, by and large, I'd trust a photographer before most other professionals.

When I teach photography classes and workshops, my students are taught how to "see"—how to translate reality into a visual image. Even when we're on a field trip and they watch me, they can't "see" the same things I do, because "seeing" is not done with a camera, it's done with the heart. I doubt that I would be as successful as I am if I spent my time figuring out how to "rip off" some merchant. I think one of our biggest advantages over other professions is striving for the best way to make photographs. It's downright contrary to a photographer's philosophy to be a cheat.

Does it not follow that we're compensated for our attitudes? Lord knows that most photographers will never be wealthy in terms of money, but then, we knew that when we went into the field. Yet we *are* compensated—in so many ways. Good photographs bring enormous pleasure to the customer and this is a thrill we witness oh so many times. This is food for the soul worth more than worldly goods.

Oh, I know, we need money too, but not one of us went into photography purely for the money. Most of us would be satisfied if we had just enough money to take the pressure off—have the bills paid, that sort of thing. We're often notoriously poor business people— not because we couldn't be good if we tried and knew how, but because we won't be, we don't want to be. We want to be photographers—good photographers, nothing more, nothing less. Most of us would be happy to go through life making others happy with our photographs.

Anytime you meet a really good photographer, you're meeting a fine person, too. It has to follow: a good photographer is good, period. I suppose a few have managed enough of the mechanics of photography to become good photographers and cheat and connive as well, but they're the exception, not the rule.

# 4 Warning! Contrived Photograph

Maybe that is what we should label some of our work. Before some government agency requires us to do so. Just lately, I have noticed a plethora of "gadgets" on the market, guaranteed to make the most ordinary of photographs into a work of art.

In a way, I am partly responsible. I specialize in a form of illustration that uses "assemblages," or multiple images. I have written many an article for magazines outlining the advantages of this or that attachment.

Now first, let me make this *perfectly clear,* if you'll pardon my use of some of this overused phrase: *all of the attachments and accessory lenses that I have mentioned are valid and useful.* I still feel that every photographer should have them. I further suggest that you need them. But not for *every* photograph! There is more to fine photographs than just the use of equipment.

There are two main sides to the professional photographer. The first is the *technical* side. The photographer must be competent technically before he or she can go on to being *creative,* the other side. Technically competent is a broad term. To the head of General Motors' Photographic Department it requires a vast amount of knowledge and experience with all types of photography. The small studio, on the other hand, needs the technical excellence that is directly pertinent to its operation.

All cameras, lenses, film, chemicals, paper and the vast array of other materials we use in photography are only *tools.* The *use* of these tools determines "technical competence." When you expose film incorrectly; when you don't balance the film properly with light balancing filters; when you simply don't understand color film and have trouble using it, you don't have technical competence.

The "content" of the photograph is the gray area between technical competence and creative photography. Content is the subject matter, the shape and form, the pleasing arrangement, the harmony of color, contrast ratio; these are half technical and half creative, but they can be learned more easily than can the pure creativity that lies behind the photograph.

*Creativity must come after technical excellence* or competence. Someone can be creative, yet not have sufficient technical knowledge or ability to translate his or her ideas into a photograph.

You can learn to be creative. I find that most photographers are looking for "instant creativity." Buy a gadget, and it will automatically make you creative? It won't! It won't. It will fool some people —the uninformed. But even they might sense the sham!

If every color laboratory catering to photographers closed up tomorrow, half the photographers in the United States would go out of business! Photographers should recognize that photography and the understanding of it is a *total* process. If you shoot color negatives, a color print must be the end result of the process.

Many photographers are dependent on the technical excellence of a good laboratory. Many lab technicians in reality save the necks of some incompetent photographers. Now don't run out and buy color printing materials and give up the labs— far from it. But you could buy Unicolor kits and do some of it yourself. Learn the processes and what can be done creatively. The experience will make you appreciate your lab, for one thing, and turn you on to one of the most rewarding areas of photography—the darkroom.

I am a believer in the idea that you are what you want to be. I believe you can learn anything you want. You don't have to have a college education to learn to be creative. The amount of material available from manufacturers for learning is enormous and most of it is free. There are hundreds of courses given by manufacturers. Almost every state has an association with monthly meetings featuring successful photographer-speakers. There is an unlimited education available to you for the asking. All it needs is your ambition!

The gadgets are only tools and should be used as such. And used where they are called for. If the success of your photograph depends on the attachment you use to make it, you have failed in content!

The easiest way to become creative is to read and study everything you can. Subscribe to all photographic magazines, leave none out—professional and amateur. Study psychology, sociology, go to night courses. Most community colleges offer courses in philosophy, creative writing, art appreciation, and so on, inexpensively. Attend your state and local associations. Above all, attend as many seminars in the field as you can afford.

Don't depend on God too much either. He made the Grand Canyon—among other things. A photograph of that on 8 × 10 film should be credited to Him, Eastman Kodak, Sinar, Schneider and the processing lab. And don't say that *you* selected the point of view and the time of day and that this photograph received a merit in the PPofA show. Send your merit to God!

When I teach, I give more credit to those photographers whose work shows *effort*. I don't mean physical effort. I mean an attempt to communicate, an attempt to say something. Even a pastoral scene can be creative and can carry, say, a *calming* message.

It is, indeed, most unfortunate that the camera can, without any help from the photographer, reproduce, faithfully, in color and automatically—simply a photograph.

There are many useful tools for the photographer, yet a dependence on tools undermines creativity. Buy them, use them, but think before you grab for something to pull you out of a bind. Ask yourself if there is a way to make a fine photograph *without* use of a gadget.

# 5 Helen and Ralph and the Kodak Color Print Replicator

Helen Curtney was a meticulous housekeeper and a compulsive note-maker. Right now, she was sitting at the kitchen table making out her shopping list and her itinerary of stops and errands.

"Let's see now—we need bread, oleo, milk, some oranges and—oh, I need some laundry bleach. Do you want me to get you anything while I'm running errands, dear?"

"Can't think of anything, dear," said her husband Ralph, peering over his morning paper. "Oh, wait a minute, look honey, since you're going to the supermarket, why don't you have those slides of Donny printed? I've marked the sizes on each so you can get the proper prints, okay?" He handed Helen a

41

group of 35mm slides and three dollar bills.

"Fine, I have some shopping there anyway, darling. By the way, did you order some 5 × 7s or 8 × 10s for the great aunts? You know they want a photograph every time Donny turns over, gets a new tooth, smiles or plays with the toys they sent him."

"Oh, yeah, they've got me trained. Every time I take photographs now, I send them some prints. It's so much easier now to get them. Not like the old days of having to go to the photo store, or the drug store or even the photo studio and wait a week for a print. Thank God for the Kodak Color Print Replicators in the supermarkets. Since they've come out, getting prints is a five-minute thing—a real snap."

"Well, I'm off . . . see you tonight, dear."

At the supermarket, Helen looked for the tall yellow and red cabinet with the familiar *Kodak* in red. There wasn't a line in front of it, so she decided to make her prints before doing the rest of her grocery shopping. These new print makers in every supermarket in the country certainly made it easy for people to get prints without waiting. Helen followed the directions on the plate: she put her slide in the slot and pushed the mechanism in; she placed the dollar bills, one at a time, in their slot and pushed twice; then she selected the size. She could have 3½ × 5s for 50 cents, 5 × 7s were a dollar and an 8 × 10 was three dollars. The machine could take any slide from 110, 126 to a 35mm. Or a negative for that matter. Helen heard the whirring and read the instructions on the plate while she waited. Her print order would take three minutes. She wondered how it was done. The age of miracles! She must ask Ralph when she got home.

Helen picked up her prints from the slot, noted that they were dry and took one of the glassine envelopes from the bin attached to the Replicator and went on about the business of grocery shopping. Later that day she asked Ralph how the machine worked.

"The Kodak Color Print Replicator was invented back in 1981," he said, looking over the high quality color prints Helen had picked up at the supermarket. "But at that time it cost about $75,000 and was quite large since it was originally made for the photo-finishing trade and high volume was one of its greatest assets; another was the fact that it eliminated an operator to select or read the transparency or negative—read in the sense of determining the color balance. The negatives or transparencies—they must be printed separately—are inserted into the machine, and a scanner, just like a TV matrix, scans the slide or negative up and down and back and forth across the area of the original. It even adjusts the filtration for subject failure—it can even read and adjust for backlighting. In fact, I have heard it told that the new scanners can make a print better than a custom printer. Anyway," he continued, "the prints are made on a new base similar to the old RC (resin coated), which was a film base and used very little chemical—much less than the old style paper bases, and doesn't need any washing at all—the chemicals are 'neutralized' rather than washed out. Of course silver is no longer used in films and paper; nowadays they use a cobalt element as a substitute."

"But didn't this upset the photo-finishing industry?" asked Helen, trying to understand Ralph's explanation of the scanner and cobalt as a silver substitute.

"Not at all. Oh, at first a couple of finishers were bent out of shape when the first Replicators went into test supermarkets, but what really happened was that their business *increased,* since almost everyone had to have either a developed slide or negative to put in the machine. The photo-finishers still supplied the original developing and printing; the KCPRs supplied *reprints.*"

"What about the thousands of photographers all over the country? Didn't they find this hurt their business? I can remember when Susan was little, we used to have to go to the portrait studio for our photography. When Donny came along, you had an Instamatic camera, and we have been taking all our own photographs. That must have hurt their business."

"Of course it has—change always hurts those who are not farsighted. Many of them went out of business, others improved their photography to the point that amateurs like me can't compete. For instance, we're still going down to Portraits, Inc., for a family group because we want big prints of a professional quality. Many of the photographers have switched to other areas of photography, areas where special expertise is still necessary."

"You mean commercial photography isn't touched by this?"

"No, quite the contrary, it didn't take art directors at the agency or even the clients long to catch onto the Replicators in the supermarkets and they too use them. Mostly for checking layouts and showing clients what they call 'comprehensives'—a mock-up of the advertisement. But the Replicators don't take the larger size films that the professionals use."

"Then the professional commercial photographer is still around?"

"In many ways, more than ever. As new inventions appear on the market, so do new uses and needs for photography. Back in the 1950s, few industries had photographic departments, but now a photo department is almost indispensable. And there are many subspecialties in photography that didn't exist years ago. I liken a great deal of these new advances in photography to the same or similar advances in duplicating. Think of Xerox, IBM and 3M, all of these can now make a color reproduction—not as good in quality as the photographic process, but any time they want to, they can make a concerted effort to achieve fine screening—maybe make a 300-line screened print. You see, the technology exists today. In fact, it existed back in 1979."

"Maybe we should get into the business and cash in on some of the new technologies. What would you suggest?" said Helen.

"Every time a new invention or a new technique is developed two things happen immediately; the first is that many people fail in business because they are too provincial—they think in immediate terms rather than of future changes. The other event that takes place is that new techniques are adapted by forward-thinking people, and a new craft is born. This is a regenerative process and is similar to what happens in nature; the weak are destroyed and only the strong survive. For every business that fails, there is a new one to take its place. For every advance in technology, there is a new craft born. This is the way of civilization and it will always be so."

"Well, I must say, since the Replicators appeared in the supermarkets, I've bought more prints than ever before, because it's so *convenient.*"

"Helen, that's the key—you just said it: it's convenient. Moreover, the prints are perfect and the public has come to expect high quality prints for a reasonable price, and that's what these Replicators do. Wish I'd thought of it."

"Ralph, anyone can succeed in business if they apply themselves, but they need more than diligence, they need to keep up with the technological changes in their field."

*Forewarned; forearmed.*

# 6 Knowledge, the Key to Success

The photographer has one big advantage over all other professions and trades—he's not dependent on the economic condition of the area where he lives, be it his community, his state or for that matter, his country. Only those photographers who *choose* to be tied to a locality must depend on it to feed their business. If his community is dominated by one, two or even three industries, then his fortunes rise and fall with theirs. For a young photographer to tie himself or herself purposely to a community could very well be the wrong way to go.

The type of photographer who remains a "local" photographer, responding only to the needs of that community, is usually not well trained in his craft.

47

He is usually a "moonlighter" turned pro, often getting into business a little too soon. His photography is what I call "focus and expose," meaning that he can do what a customer tells him to do. He lights with flash or quartz lamps, focuses his camera and exposes the film reasonably well. He may advertise as a "creative" photographer, hire employees, and do enough business to pay his bills. If making money is his criterion for professionalism and success, then he is successful.

Most such photographers are stymied when they really have to perform with imagination. Whenever they have to go beyond "focus and expose," they're lost. At first, they try the usual ploys—a new camera, a special lens, that fancy filter that so-and-so uses— or they land in a sea of gadgets that will make their photographs "different." A whole segment among the photographic manufacturers exists just to feed the needs of such photographers. They run from one planned disaster to the next.

It's these same photographers who become so vocal at association meetings and write letters to the professional magazines complaining loudly about department store photographic prices, demanding protection or licensing or unionizing or who ask the association to protect them in some way from the competition. If a professional is worried about competition, he's the problem, not his competition. It's ludicrous for him to make such complaints, since doing so identifies him as not quite good enough to be above the competition. If you are such a person, even though you have a right to be a photographer, you must recognize that you need help, unless, of course, you are happy with your lot. In that case, discussion is ended.

Generally, such competition-shy photographers look through magazines and envy the real professionals who are gaining fame and fortune. They often look at the photographs, searching for the "trick," wondering what filter he used, what gadget made the picture good. Yet, the key isn't a new lens, a filter or some special camera, but a new way of life, a way that goes beyond "focus and expose," beyond gadgets and tricks. The secret is *knowledge.* Isn't it always, in any field of endeavor?

Knowledge is the key that can unlock your career, but unlike most other professions and trades, the photographer not only has to learn to make excellent photographs but he must first learn to be imaginative. It is the quality of a photographer's thoughts, his sensitivity, his artistic flair and his empathy with the environment that—added to his control of photographic techniques—makes glorious images that all can enjoy. But, even with these first two elements of knowledge—technique and imagination—he still may fail. The third key is marketing. As much as many of us would like to remain "pure" artists, whatever that means, we must be experts in the game of money management and in the marketplace. Make no mistake, without success here, even before the other two, you will fail as a total photographer. The knowledge of selling is of the utmost importance, yet many look at it with disdain and a certain amount of contempt, calling it crass commercialism. Well, it is commercialism. You'd best get used to it and fast, because unless you find someone to do your selling for you, you're going to have to do it.

So it's knowledge of *creative imagination* coupled with knowledge of *photographic techniques* and, finally, married to knowledge of *creative marketing* that insures financial success. How do you obtain knowledge? Aside from the obvious assertion that pursuing four years of college leading to a degree in Fine Arts—Photography, followed by one year or so of a professional photographic school, then spending a year or so as an assistant in a large studio, is the way to go, there are still other ways. The two best are, first, to take courses in the humanities, psychology, philosophy and business and marketing. Such courses are offered by the evening extension divisions of universities and community colleges. The second way is to attend seminars and workshops given by recognized professionals.

Selecting the right courses at colleges and universities is not difficult since you know pretty well what you want and what your own intellect needs. It's harder to choose the right professional seminars or workshops, since they usually have no structured course outlines, which makes them difficult to analyze. Their big advantage is that the course time is concentrated, usually no more than two weeks, provided the day is oriented around actual work and study rather than socializing. Socializing is my main complaint with professional conventions; too little time is given to the actual study seminars.

Any good workshop or seminar should offer instruction in the technique, imagination and marketing, unless it is so specialized that you want to attend for a specific subject.

Most knowledge received in crash courses is useless unless applied. The difference between the structured university courses and workshops is that at the university you are required to prove what you have learned by a homework assignment or a comprehensive test, or both. Testing is still the best way to evaluate the performance of a student.

Self-teaching is also possible, but only for a few photographers who are self-starters. It takes an enormous amount of discipline to control yourself so that you can define your objectives, plan and select the material to study, do the studying, test yourself, review your lessons and apply the lessons learned, and then to evaluate the efficacy of the entire project before starting the process all over again. Without advice—and who can offer advice to someone in this situation—it's doubly difficult. Still, it can be done and has been done.

Where to start? Perhaps our heritage will give us the clue. Two hundred years ago, a prospective member of a profession was required to read and read and read. After that schooling, he usually served an apprenticeship with a professional. Mind you, I'm not talking about practitioners of crafts—the cabinetmaker, the candlestick maker, the silversmith and the photographer—I'm talking about the *professionals*—the doctor, lawyer, apothecary, architect and similar masters. After serving for a year, in some cases, or longer, in others, the apprentice applied to the peer group for entry and was tested by that group. If he was found wanting, he returned to his apprenticeship; if he was found competent, he was given professional status.

How different it is today. You can buy a camera and some equipment and just go into business, whether you are capable or not. Yet even for the unschooled, the keys to expertise are available. But yet, the clue is there. Knowledge is reading and understanding. Techniques can be learned by reading about them and trying them out. Even creativity can be *learned.* Sensitivity and empathy are more difficult but it is possible to learn even these things. The marketing of photography also can be learned. Without the desire to improve, none of this is possible. With fierce ambition, the drive to excel, and the need for gratification, all is possible.

You may want to think about this:
Abraham Lincoln spent only one year in school—
under the tutelage of five different teachers—
and that man authored the *Gettysburg Address.*

# 7 Books, Books and More Books

I grew up with *The Adventures of Tom Swift, The Last of the Mohicans, Robinson Crusoe, King Arthur and the Knights of the Round Table,* the Teenie-Weenie People, Robin, Pooh, Piglet and Eeyore and many, many other fascinating books and their inhabitants. Apparently, I was anti-social from the time I first learned to read. Whenever everything became too much for me, I went into my room, locked the door and read. Reading was my escape from the realities of life. I didn't have such a bad life; it was just that my adventurous spirit needed the soaring fantasies of the make-believe world. It is said that a reader "suspends his disbelief" when he reads fiction. I think that I suspended reality or, perhaps,

53

disbelieved life and lived instead in the fantasy world created by the antics of my book characters.

In the 1920s, reading was a basic habit of my life. Radio was in its infancy and there was no TV. Most families of my acquaintance played games, put together jigsaw puzzles, or read. Since children went to bed at around eight or nine, we were in our rooms long before we were sleepy. So there was a certain thrill to reading *Tom Swift in the Land of the Giants* by flashlight under the blanket. Reading was one of those secret pleasures I was accustomed to early on in life. Lucky are those of us who found the joy and pleasure of reading while young. Reading is a habit that has literally opened the doors of opportunity for me.

I was also blessed with relatives whose idea of a present for a small child was a book, although I must admit I didn't *always* think so since some of my friends had toys that seemed more exciting. I realize now that I was lucky to receive books. I had toys, too, but it was my books that became my friends.

Today, books have even more value than they did then: they're also the source of much of my present income—and I don't mean my own several published books. I use books to create photographs. Until recently, I had not realized how much I depended on books for inspiration in creating photographic images. I was aware, as we all no doubt are, that *instructional* books are vital to the furtherance of our professional lives. We've all purchased many books so as to learn something more about photography, but how much are books credited as being part of the *creative* process?

I stopped being "open to the public" about 10

years ago. I had changed my photographic business from performing for a client—making a photograph that he or she wanted—to speculative selling, where I make a photograph to my liking and then attempt to find a client for it. That's really an oversimplification, but it is essentially true. This meant that instead of carrying a product into my studio and placing it on a background (I was a commercial photographer), I now went into my living room and "thought" about a photograph. The switch in the approach improved all my photography. The fact that the phone didn't constantly ring, that no employees were around to be kept busy, that people were not forever coming to the door for appointments—all these absences wiped away distraction, the enemy of creative thought. I remember some of the earlier days of simply staring at a product or some other object and reflecting on the best way to photograph it. My first response would be the old-fashioned, simplistic method of turning a light on the object, but soon I began to pull books down off the shelves and browse. It wasn't long after that that I began to realize I had much gold on those shelves in the form of inspiration from looking at other photographs.

As years went by, I became better and better at what I was doing. Fewer and fewer people stopped by, and once again, I became the little boy in his room with his books. I took more time, and I became more selective. I found some books to be more useful than others, so I started to group them by their value as research tools for photographic assignments. I attached new values to books you wouldn't ordinarily dream had so much to offer. It wasn't long before I started to search for more books—this time keeping in mind my newly defined requirements. My library grew. Eventually, I expanded my research library to include books that inspired me but weren't photographic books. These were books on art, but only certain kinds of art. I started to study the popular paintings of artists to see if there wasn't something I had missed while looking at them at school. There most certainly was! I can't for the life of me understand what I thought I was looking at when I went to college. Suddenly, "famous" paintings made new sense to me, and they inspired me to push at the borders of photographic discipline. Benton showed me how to use my 21mm lens, Monet showed me how to "see" color, Manet showed me that ordinary people do ordinary things that need to be photographed. Even Dali provoked me to experiment, while Magritte and Escher practically blew my mind. Seurat and his pointillism inspired profitable ideas. The list of my benefactors is virtually endless.

Of all the books on photography, perhaps one set has above all others been rewarding to me—*Photographis,* a collection of books published in Switzerland on an annual basis. They contain the best illustration photographs from all over the world. They are expensive—about $38 per copy—but financially I am in their debt. *Variations I* and *II,* by my friend René Groebli in Zürich, were the start of my of my change of viewpoint. Soon I was collecting all the best books of famous photographers: Beaton, Boje, Cartier-Bresson, Dedienes, Duncan, Glyck, Halsman, Haskins, Karsh, Keppler, Marynowkz, Paine, Rawlings, Reedy, Skrebneski, Steichen and Uelmann, to name a few. And these were just photographic, not how-to, books. I have hundreds of how-to books, and they prove useful, but for pure inspiration, something to stir the creative juices, I'll take the "coffee-table" book over the how-to any day. Strangely, one often hears of photographers passing up artistic books in favor of craft books. Too bad. Seurat has taught me more about images than any photographic book, except perhaps Groebli's *Variations I.* (There are an awful lot of weird snapshot-photo books being published today—but they turn me off.)

Among craft books, I can't sing enough praises of John Hedgecoe's *The Photographer's Handbook.* If I were ever asked to name a one-volume, all-inclusive book on the craft of photography, this would be the one I'd recommend for the amateur or professional. The Life Library of Photography series would be the collection I'd recommend most highly in the area of how-to. (And I do hope you'll forgive an author's conceit if I mention two of my own previous books, *Photography for the Professionals* and *Creative Color Photography.*)

Obtaining some of these books can be quite difficult. How-to books are very accessible, but not so much the coffee-table variety. Many publishers feel that how-to books sell better, which may unfortunately be true—despite the fact that photographic books contain so much from which to learn. Hastings House carries most of the exotic picture books; you can request to be placed on their photographic book mailing list. *Variations* and *Photographis* both come from Hastings. Other photo books come from Amphoto, but you'll have to obtain a catalogue to find them. Publishers' Clearing House issues a list of remaindered books once or twice a year. I scan these catalogues for picture book gems that can be had at astonishingly reduced prices. *The New York Times Book Review* has classified ads in its back pages for bookstores that specialize in old photographic books. A good book club, such as the Popular Photography Book Club, is an excellent source of real bargains.

How do I use these books? I usually use the *Photographis* books when I am trying to design a photograph. I peruse each copy, which takes the better part of an hour. I write down some of the images and the pages, and I analyze the "concept" of the product or idea. This is important. I must know the photographer's concept. Usually, a photograph will give me an idea of how to approach my product or concept. The choice of lens, the selection of depth, the type and control of lighting, all of these help me in choosing ideas for my own concept. I do very little outright copying, not only because I don't believe in it but, more important, because my product, idea need or service never seems ideally to fit someone else's format.

On the other hand, the works of great artists have contributed enormously to what I do. Magritte and Escher have been greatly useful to me for their outrageous imaginations. Their images are so forceful, they seem to smack me full in the face. Degas' *The Glass of Absinthe* showed me how to use foreground. Vermeer's *The Cook* has much to say about modern lighting techniques. I've always wanted to photograph a group of people on a tree limb, as suggested by Goya's *Strange Folly.* Munch's *Anxiety* is another kind of use of the wide-angle lens, as is Benton's *July Hay.* Duchamp's *Bride Descending the Staircase* has inspired many of my photographs. And for sheer power of imagining, where would I be if I had not seen Michelangelo's depiction of the creation of man?

These are just a few of the outstanding images that have changed my photography. So much can be gained by reading. As they say, a mind is a terrible thing to waste. So's a good eye.

# 8 The New Breed

It used to be that the beginning photographer moon-lighted until his extra-curricular income was about 50 percent of his primary income; then he'd open a studio or work out of his home. If his photography grew up in an urban environment, he might have gone the newspaper-photo-journalism route. Of course, these are basic representations but by and large this is the general way most photographers began their careers. The earlier group worked for studios or laboratories, moonlighted and then got into one of the above.

I see this changing. Recent talks with many young photographers have convinced me that they want little part of the traditional "studio," with its expensive fixtures, trappings and equipment. They see the studio owner as one who makes little net income, with too much of his or her gross going to enormous rents and overhead, and facing labor problems and perhaps even government intervention.

The independence of this new generation of photographers comes from today's lifestyle. The members of this generation feel less responsibility to follow the old ways; they want little dependence on the fixed location; they want to "float," to earn their photographic living by making it coincide with their new lifestyle. They may very well be 'on the right track.

Energy is definitely a major consideration in starting any business today. If customers are restricted by shortages, then the photographer must go to the customer—but maybe not in the way you might first think of. Maybe the best way to sell is to do it by mail. At least by mail the photographer is not restricted to the general locality or the stretch of his gas line. In fact, by using the U.S. Post Office delivery systems, the photographer can expand his customers to include the world.

The world has been shrinking for years and will most likely continue to do so as long as communications improve. Making a transatlantic telephone call is, in most cases, as simple as making a call within your own state. You can dial most European countries directly, and these calls are less expensive than you may think. Calling London costs only $3.60 for the first three minutes; calling Paris costs $6.75, as does Rome. I've paid more for calls within the United States.

In 1969 I went to Europe and made contact with a number of representatives to handle my work. I now have my "European Connection" so firmly entrenched that a sizeable portion of my income comes from clients outside the United States. This segment of my work is growing because the reevaluation of the Swiss franc, German mark, the French franc and the British pound, with the corresponding devaluation of the American dollar, has made it profitable for foreign countries to "buy American." In my own small way, I'm helping the balance of payments. There are other advantages to dealing with Europe. For one thing the competition is less intense; few Americans bother to sell in Europe, mostly because they don't know where and how to make the "connection" or they have an inborn suspicion that "foreigners" will cheat you. My experience is quite the contrary; any cheating, either by using my images without pay or neglecting to return them to me, has been far more prevalent in the United States than in Europe. In addition, what one is paid by European clients is about on a par with what one is paid in the United States.

Just as the American model is popular with European magazines and corporate advertisers, so is the American photographer. He may be little known in the United States, but in Europe his reputation can grow quickly. My own career is a prime example: I was known in Europe before I became known in the United States. A European flavor to your portfolio doesn't hurt either—it in fact gives you that "continental air."

In my Creative Color Workshops, I suggest that photographers contact all popular European magazines and major corporations. Make contact by sending 35mm color transparencies with a stamped, self-addressed envelope for convenience in returning your work. Remember, though, that U.S. stamps are not acceptable; buy the equivalent in International Coupons at your local post office. You're judged not by the size of your studio, by how many employees you have, by what ribbons you hang around your neck or by what awards you may have received—but strictly by the quality and efficacy of your work. And when you get right down to it, what better way is there than to be judged by the quality of your work?

The new breed of photographer is trained on a "need to know" basis. I would recommend to anyone wishing to become a professional photographer to get a four-year college degree in Liberal Arts and then to take a series of especially good workshops with specific professionals. Add copious reading, and you've got a fine professional photographer. I worry that so many of the traditional photographic schools tend to perpetuate a system of photography that is no longer appropriate in this fast-moving world. There is little individuality among professionals. Much of this similarity comes from the attempt to mimic the judges or the award-winning prints exhibited. Sort of a self-fulfilling prophesy—maybe even a death wish.

Darwin's theory of the Survival of the Fittest explains how the unfit, the inept and the lethargic are weeded out. Photography is no profession for the lazy or the indolent. I used to say that if you couldn't cut the mustard as a professional photographer, you should go pump gas. Now you can't even do that.

# 9 Provincialism –and the Ways out of It

My dictionary defines provincialism as ". . . narrowness of mind, ignorance or the like resulting from provincial life without exposure to cultural or intellectual activity . . ." That's also a pretty good definition of many professional photographers, especially the part about "narrowness of mind." By that I don't mean ignorance of intellectual activity as much as being narrow-minded when it comes to the scope of their business in photography.

Just after World War II, professional photographers other than photo-journalists and freelancers thought of themselves essentially as studio owners having a fixed place of business and supplying photographic services to the community. Most of these studio photographers were generalists, practicing many kinds of photography, including portraiture, weddings—both formal and candid photos—children, animals, and some nebulous form of commercial photography including some product photography, construction progress photography, corporation activity (usually public relations), identification, passports, school proms and anything else you might think of. According to the latest U.S. Census, there are over 100,000 of these studios still flourishing in the United States. But the vast majority are not flourishing, far from it. Most of them are just above or at the poverty level.

It was originally thought that the continuing increase in population would improve the lot of these photographers, but that hasn't proved to be so, probably because of the growth of shopping centers and discount stores, which do an annual business of almost $1,000,000,000 in child portraiture. The erosion of gross business from Mom and Pop studios by these mass-production portrait corporations is enormous. Surprisingly, their work is not shoddy—far from it; some of it is better than many of the studio-printed portraits I've seen.

Studio photographers look for high density/traffic locations, or at least they used to. Recently, the home-studio has seemed a more practical adventure, but still the feeling is that you're serving the community no matter where you are. I feel that this philosophy may be fine for the successful, but I'd suggest that photographers investigate tearing down the fences and eliminating their mental borders and start recognizing that they're entitled to sell their photography world-wide.

Freelancers have known this for years and regularly solicit work by advertising in European journals and mailing sets of their work, usually in the form of 35mm color transparencies, either to agents and representatives or directly to prospective clients. Their problem has been that they don't really know how or where to start. Perhaps I can help.

Many areas are dominated by one or perhaps two large industrial complexes. Most small businesses in such areas are totally dependent on the economic climate of their area. If Corporation X sneezes, everyone in the community takes out his handkerchief. If you are in such a situation, your business may suffer through no fault of your own. If a studio is dependent on the thousands of workers at a plant, and the workers go on strike or are laid off, causing an economic depression in the community, the studio necessarily suffers.

Such problems do not effect you so severely if your market is world-wide. If one area does become temporarily depressed, you sell in another. You are actually working in all markets at the same time. Incidentally, you need no expensive studio; you could work out of an apartment, a garage or a basement since all of your work is mailed and you never see the client. You need no "100 percent location" at $20 a square foot, which is what many studios cost nowadays. No need for fancy employees, who get sick, need vacations or come due for raises. Aren't you tired of working two days out of each week for your employees and one day for the federal government? Three days a week you aren't working for yourself. The rest of the week is divided between paperwork at your desk and visiting with sales people. Didn't you go into photography to be a photographer and to take photographs that please *you?*

The solution to all this is to get back to being a photographer. There is one major change required in your thinking, though; you can't depend on customers coming to you—you have to send your work to prospects. This means you're going to have to depend on your own initiative; you're going to have to be self-disciplined.

What type of photography is wanted? Perhaps the best way to answer that one is first to tell you what isn't wanted. Clients don't want scenics, travel or sports photographs; nothing ordinary. This just about closes the door for you? Not really. Clients need *imaginative* photographs, which is fortunate, since imaginative photographs are made from basic photographs taken with *thought.* Let me give you an example: find a flower such as a lily; photograph it from very close—fill the frame on a 35 mm. Now find a lovely young lady and photograph her in the buff on a pure white background, back to you with her hands over her head, body twisted to match the flow of the lily's petals. After processing, combine the two and rephotograph on Ektachrome Slide Duplicating Film #5071 and make at least ten *originals.* You read correctly: the new image, combined, is an original made up of two parts. Now *that* photograph has marketability, but before you start mailing you'll need at least twenty good images.

Try another: photograph a class ring close up, sideways on white. Make another photograph of a couple on the beach arm-in-arm. Combine those. Or photograph an ear, full frame, then photograph a nude reading a magazine and superimpose her within the long curve of the ear.

I call the individual photographs "elements." You can get more precise information from my book *Creative Color Photography* (Amphoto).

*Marketing* these photographs is the heart of the game and almost all prospective clients are listed in one book: *Photography Market Place,* edited by Fred W. McDarrah and published by the R. R. Bowker Company. Simply pick out a greeting card manufacturer, a record company, a match book manufacturer and seven more *diversified* companies. Send each company a set of your twenty slides along with a stamped, self-addressed envelope. Remember, if you don't act professionally, you might not be given consideration. (If you don't send SASE, they can, and some will, dump your slides into the wastebasket.) It will probably take a year of mailings after you've made your photographs before you start making sales. But the sales lead to assignments or requests for more slides. In two years you could have a steady income of about $10,000 a year from just this one project. The trick is to mail the slides to another prospect the *same day they come back.* Keep the work moving constantly. It will even make you feel better.

You've no doubt seen many a photograph in magazines and thought, "Hell, I could make a picture as good as that." You probably could but you didn't! And you didn't sell it! Don't just claim to have beautiful photographs in your studio/darkroom or wherever. Don't just complain that business is bad—it always is. Don't cry away your life. Do something.

# 10 The Photographer and the Economy

**W**e've been so preoccupied with the rising cost of almost everything that we've lost sight of some important changes in our economy that will affect every photographer. Many items have gone down in price. Think of pocket calculators, quartz wrist watches, adding machines, tape recorders, simple power tools and cameras. *Cameras?* Yes, even cameras have dropped in price over the years. I can remember paying around $300 for a Contax "S," one of the earliest single lens reflex cameras in the early 1950s, and it wasn't nearly as sophisticated as today's. Twenty-five dollars in 1950 would buy a simple Black & Decker electric drill that today wouldn't cost you more than $8.95 at the neighborhood discount store. Many other

69

products will become less expensive in the future.

Why do products drop in price at the same time that they are improved? Doesn't this seem strange in the face of rising costs of labor and raw materials? The real reason is the combination of *supply* and *demand,* the fundamental basis of a capitalist system. As newly invented products and services catch on, manufacturers gear up for *mass production* and this causes prices to lower. The consumer benefits with better products at reduced prices. For an example of the effect of one small invention, think of the miniaturization of electronics and how it has revolutionized the manufacture of almost everything. We should all pay homage to the "chip," an electronic board that can fit on your fingertip and contains as much as a billion "bits," or pieces of information. Don't open your new SLR, but the chances are that it's loaded with electronics. Incidentally, that's one reason why it costs so much to repair. The repairer can't get by with just being a good mechanic; he must be an electronic technician too. The magic words today are *solid state.*

So what do you think will come down in price regardless of the price of oil and many other raw materials as well as labor? And what does this mean to the average photographer and his or her business? Quite a lot really—we just have to think ahead and try to anticipate what is going on in the economy, and then use it to our advantage.

Let's examine lifestyles. Today's inventions make it possible to travel in four or less hours to Europe or across this continent. You no longer need to think of your customers as local. Why not serve a customer in France or Great Britain? I do. I have clients in Denmark, Japan, Germany, France, Italy and Great Britain. In my Creative Color Workshops I have one photographer from India and one from Australia. My lifestyle has changed because I took advantage of new inventions and different ways of living.

We all use these new inventions. I am typing the manuscript of this chapter on an IBM Correcting Selectric II typewriter. I don't have to type a finished or "corrected" error-free copy—everything I type is recorded on tape on a Savin 900 Word Master Computer hooked to the typewriter. When I make editing corrections I do it on the control panel of the Savin and then reprint the final fresh copy by pushing an "auto" button. I sit here and change the paper. Again, I am able to communicate with hundreds of photographers with this machine. So, my workstyle has changed.

When I take notes for my books, I use a Minicorder, a form of a tape recorder you can put in your pocket. These notes are then played back on the typewriter mentioned above. Look around you. Sit down with a pad and pencil some evening and write down all the items that have changed your lifestyle and when you get to photography you'll begin to see that you must change your photographic business style or you might find yourself out of business.

In 1776, the world's population was about 800 million; it took 4 million years to reach this figure. Just 200 years later the world had 4.1 *billion* people. In the next 38 years, within the life span of any photographer presently 50 or younger, the world's population is supposed to rise to 8.2 billion people, or just double the 1976 figure. This means that our economy will be increasingly people oriented. The coming market for professional photographic services is so staggering that it defies the imagination. Product photography will increase 10 times in the next 35 years. Mass-production portraiture is going to sail right off every chart or graph. But, this will tend to lower *the price,* if we follow the laws of supply and demand. Those photographers improving themselves and their studios to separate their work from that of the mass-production studios will be able to tap the new markets of family photographs, providing they will have kept pace with the new technology as it becomes available and are able to make bigger and better portraits.

Actually, what will result will be widening gaps among photographers. Most small Mom and Pop studios will be forced to the wall by increasing prices and will be unable to compete with the big mass-production portrait and school companies now serving large stores in shopping centers and malls. The more successful studios will be those that take immediate advantage of changes in technology in photography, who constantly update their equipment and rejuvenate their own photographic abilities. This will require a constant monitoring of the changes in lifestyle and the invention of new products.

Provincialism will be the death knell of those photographers who live in the old-fashioned ethic of a downtown location and who will tend to serve only those clients they can reach with their eyes.

As the world grows smaller you will find European photographers tapping the American markets. They already are—just as I tap their markets. There is no place on earth that I don't feel I can serve as a photographer. You can serve the same world.

It's a shame, but there are few ways to upgrade yourself. So you must be a self-starter, capable of teaching yourself by reading and attending work-shops and seminars. More important, you're going to have to broaden your horizons, look around you at the changes in lifestyles. Where do people shop? Since discretionary income *appears* to be dropping, are you competing with the local ski shop, camera shop, or whatever hobby there is for your clients' luxury dollars? The commercial photographer must search for clients everywhere.

To say that new markets are being invented daily is not to exaggerate. Think of a new use for your photography every day, see new people, investigate new markets, look for new products to photograph, watch the new lifestyles. There will always be new cameras, new techniques to learn—these are all new ways by which you must make money and improve your own lifestyle. Don't be part of your problem, be the solution to it.

# 11 Hypnosis, Transcendenta Meditation and Other Goodies

Thirty years ago, I practiced hypnosis professionally on the stage. This experience and my training in
psychology have stood me in good stead in my work
as a photographer throughout these last 30 years, but
perhaps the most important thing I learned from my
practice of hypnosis is an awareness that the human
mind uses so little of its actual capacity.

One of my "tricks" was to put a subject into a
trance and station him or her at the back of the room,
with the audience between us. Then, with a couple of
witnesses standing next to me, I'd whisper a double
number that was barely audible to the witnesses and
not heard at all by the audience, but repeated loud
and clear by the subject. The impression was that I

had, through mental telepathy, transmitted a thought to my subject, when in reality all I had done was to utilize the full hearing capability of my subject—a capability that God gave us all.

All humans have five known senses: sight, smell, touch, taste and hearing. Each of these senses can be and is used consciously and subconsciously at the same time. For instance, when you're not straining to hear something, you hear subconsciously; at the same time, you are seeing, touching, smelling and tasting. Should a strange sight appear before your eyes, your attention is drawn to it and the other four senses drop to the subconscious level while the attention is concentrated on the sight. But the other four senses don't go to sleep or even shut off. If, while your attention was on the sight, your hearing was alerted by a strange sound, your attention would be drawn to it and your former single-sense (sight) concentration would now be split between two—sight and sound.

There are situations where you can become acutely aware of all five of your senses: for a woman, natural childbirth is one; for a soldier, battle.

Any one of these five senses can be used more fully than we normally do. It has been proved that for normal functions we use only 30 percent of the total capability available in any one sense. In itself it is astonishing that we use so little of our abilities. Now substitute "abilities" for "capabilities" and you can begin to see what I am talking about.

In my stage shows, the "key," or trick, was to use the workings of the mind so that I could get my subject not to 30 percent of his or her ability, but to a full 100 percent. How did I do this? In hypnotic trances it is possible to "put to sleep" any of the senses by suggestion. The hypnotist dulls the conscious mind by suggestion and substitutes his or her own conscious mind for the subject's control center. Once that is done, he can freely make suggestions to the subconscious mind *that will be obeyed* by the subject since the subject's conscious mind thinks that it is obeying itself. The hypnotist suggests that, "you cannot see anything that I don't want you to see—close your eyes and see nothing," or "you cannot feel anything," etc., etc. The idea is to place all the senses but one into a state of limbo and force the subject to concentrate on that one sense, in this case, hearing. Now the sense of hearing is further increased by the suggestion that the subject has super-hearing (which he or she does not) and, further, since none of the other senses is interfering or drawing attention, the subject's concentration is highly focused on hearing.

As a result, the subject can hear better than you can—or better than you *think* you can. Getting the proper distance between the subject and the audience and my voice is a matter of experience. I only need to go just beyond the audience's ability to hear. Even when they are told to concentrate they can't come near my subject's ability since all of their senses are working, some at the conscious level. *Violà!* You have an apparent trick.

This is a roundabout way to point out to you that you have much more ability as a person than you think you have. Let me show you how an even greater capability can be achieved. I call it "sense selection." You might call it concentration, but whatever it is called, it can be developed. In fact, it is often developed by athletes and some so-called mental giants.

Nature has provided us with an aid we don't think about. If we were to learn to use it, we could accomplish more. The adrenal glands are two small glands, one on top of each kidney. Each gland has two parts; the cortex and the medulla. The cortex secretes some 38 hormones and the medulla produces the hormone adrenalin. The two main functions of the adrenal cortex are to control the salt and water content of the body and to regulate the sugar and protein metabolism.

The medulla, which produces adrenalin, is immediately activated when you become angry, frightened or excited. This produces chemical changes that prepare the body for action. The adrenalin pours into the bloodstream and is carried to every part of the body; it causes the heart to beat faster and increases blood pressure. In turn, muscles are able to work faster and longer, which is why a person who is frightened can run faster than one who isn't. The blood supply to the brain is also increased.

What does all this have to do with you as a photographer? Quite a lot: if you can learn to auto-suggest, you can increase the use of a sense you may need at a certain time. If you can learn to get excited just before a picture session, you can trigger adrenalin and have it work for you. For example, I have lectured to thousands of people in audiences all over the world. I've had my own TV talk show, yet just before I go on I have to "psyche" myself up and shoot the adrenalin. This used to happen naturally, but my senses have become jaded through the years because I frequently speak before groups. I've lost the nervousness that once triggered the adrenalin flow. Nervousness before shooting has advantages; it sharpens your mind. If you're too relaxed you won't think.

You've heard of the benefits of Transcendental Meditation. TM is great if you need a session devoted to creative thinking, not doing. The doing comes after the TM session.

TM does relax the mind, slows the pulse rate and is quite beneficial to a calm outlook. I have taken some courses in it and find that it is so close to auto-suggestion as practiced by me and taught by me for that matter, that for all intents and purposes, the two are the same thing. When working on an annual report or some creative assignment, I prefer the concentration I can develop through auto-suggestion. When I'm working, I also need the opposite effect. I need the heightened awareness and perception I get with a dose of adrenalin, so I "psyche" myself as any athlete or performer does and shoot.

Apparently, the good Lord knew what He was doing when He engineered us. He determined that all our senses should be available in abundance and, further, that should we lose one of the five, the others would compensate for the deficiency, bringing our sensitivity back to its normal level. A blind person can hear better because more of his or her concentration is placed on hearing. The hearing isn't improved so much as it is used to a fuller degree. If you think your capabilities are limited, you might find that you simply don't use your own full capacity. If I may quote from a marvelous book, *The Web and the Rock,* by Thomas Wolfe,

> ... if a man has talent and cannot use it,
> he has failed. If he has a talent and uses only

half of it, he has partly failed. If he has a talent and learns somehow to use the whole of it, he has gloriously succeeded, and won a satisfaction and a triumph few men ever know . . .

# 12 Fame and Pride

When I was 13 years old I sold a photograph of a bull mastiff for five dollars and my photographic career was off to a fine start. I remember my elation at the sale. Up until that day I had assumed that photography was a costly hobby and found that it took all my after-school earnings for such things as Super Sensitive Ortho film, Azo paper, MQ tubes of developer (used for both the development of the film and paper), a bag of sodium thiosulphate (hypo).

It had all started the year before when my scoutmaster asked if I'd like to stay after a meeting, develop some film and make some prints. Curiosity or boredom, I don't know which, led me to stay (better'n going home to homework). He soon taught me to unroll the film, discard the paper backing and hold a curl in the film, raise and lower my arms so that the film passed through a tray of developer. It took a long time and my arms soon grew tired, but lo and behold, a gray-green image appeared on the emulsion side. My scoutmaster-instructor decided to rinse the film and then he took over for the same up/down motion for the fixing. Printing turned out to be more fun. The dried negatives were placed in a print frame in contact with Azo paper, exposed to the light, then processed in trays under the red glow of the safelight. Prints were dried on black ferrotype tins. They often "popped" off with little round areas of unglazed spots. So, I backed into photography by doing darkroom work before I ever took a picture. It wasn't long after that meeting night that I got my first Kodak, a Boy Scout folding camera that, I believe, took a 127 film.

A year later, I was in Central Park (my home in those days was New York City) taking photographs. I was always very careful and took all day to decide what to photograph. One roll of film produced eight negatives; the price was about 65 cents. That was 1930 and money was scarce. Nor did Mrs. Murphy pay young Robin much for filling the ash barrels and putting them out on the sidewalk. Selling subscriptions to *Colliers* had already earned me a great shiny red Columbia bike but my small circle of friends and relatives had been exhausted. Mrs. Murphy's 50 cents a day represented two hours in the morning and two at night, and hard work, too, for everybody burned coal in those days.

The first enlarger was a Federal of some kind and that came as a Christmas gift. Hints I gave left and right supplied me with things like a print frame, black enamel drying tins, trays and, of course, one ruby red bulb.

Anyway, I was in Central Park, my favorite playground, when I saw a large dog sitting in the sun, his owner was reading on a park bench. The mastiff and I were already acquainted. He long ago had learned to tolerate and maybe even enjoy my gentle scratching behind his ears and my constant stream of childish, nonsensical talk. I lay on the grass and carefully took aim. The camera was on "I" for instant. He blinked at the "click" but otherwise took no notice of my foolishness. The next week I showed an 8 × 10 on Opal G to his owner and for some unaccountable reason she gave me five dollars—she could have had the print for 50 cents. My career was launched.

That was 45 years ago and I have clicked off enough shutters to have earned a million and a half dollars. Not much has stuck to my fingers but I must say I've enjoyed most of it and I still have the same thrill seeing a print come up in the developer. Besides, it beats hauling ashes.

My original daydreams included becoming a famous photographer whose work would be recognized the world over. People would buy my photography and museums would hang it; I would have independent shows with reviews in newspapers and magazines. My name would be known everywhere and would be synonymous with photography. Well, most of that small boy's dream never did quite come true. But there were other compensations.

After World War II, I did a stint at Kodak in Rochester and then returned to Connecticut where I had been stationed for a portion of the war. I opened a studio. I did everything and anything photographic. I guess I'll always remember some of the portraits I took in those days. The thrill of having a family really like a portrait I had taken; the pleasure on a young schoolgirl's face as she viewed her prints; the fun of doing a wedding, knowing I was taking good photographs; but best of all, I remember an incident that to this day still compensates me far more than fame or money ever could.

A German couple in their late 70s came in for a sitting. He was a retired college professor. They entered arm in arm as though he was escorting her. Then I realized that in reality, she was holding his arm, steadying him. They wanted a portrait of the two of them. While she was in the dressing room fixing her hair, he confided to me that he was dying of cancer and wanted a good photograph before he died. His candor shocked me. He also told me that they had been married over 50 years and that their children had all grown and gone their respective ways. He wanted portraits for them. When she came out he went in to comb his hair and she confided that he was dying of cancer but that he didn't know that she knew and that she wanted an especially nice photograph. I was inspired. I think I worked the hardest I have ever worked, to do the best job I could do. A few weeks later she came in and ordered the prints and again he appeared to be escorting her with Old-World courtliness. The love that existed between these two was extremely touching to me, to my receptionist, to my retoucher and to my darkroom man, all of whom had met them by this time. Another week or two went by and the couple came in to pick up the final prints. We all managed to be around when they looked at the photographs. They were delighted. Naturally, I was pleased and proud.

A few months went by. Then the man's wife returned. She came in alone and told me that he had died; I was genuinely sorry, but she did not seem upset. She asked me to take a photograph of her alone for her children as she did not expect to live long. Once again, I was shocked, but I did a fine portrait, which she gave to her children. Sure enough, a few months later I heard that she had died.

In my studio we talked about that couple for years—about their respect for each other, the obvious love that had so deeply affected us, and the fact that they both knew about their imminent deaths. We all agreed that those photographs were the best that we had been involved in and we made sets for ourselves to remind us of the real purpose of our photography. I still have mine, and I imagine the others still have theirs.

Those photographs will never hang in museums nor will I ever include them in a show. Most present-day critics of photography would pass them by as "ordinary," certainly not worthy of extra attention. But for me those photographs taught me my real worth. Hidden now from the world in my file, the portraits remain a very special and valuable lesson in just what fame means and doesn't mean.

I shall always have pride in the photograph of my bull mastiff and so many portraits and other photographs whose real worth lies in their emotional value to those who own them—and those who made them.

# 13 A Fairy Tale, Perhaps a Fable?

Once upon a time, long, long ago, far off and away from the bustling crowds of cities, there lived a man named Joe. Now Joe was simple folk, he neither wanted nor needed much. He was happy just the way he was, working in the fields and his vegetable garden, tending to the few animals that supplied him with milk and sometimes meat, although often as not his animals became his friends and when it came time to slaughter, Joe just couldn't do it. Joe, who was a bachelor, had a dog who was his faithful friend and constant companion, Jeremiah. Jeremiah wasn't much to look at, being a mongrel dog with a coat that looked for all the world like an old raccoon coat worn by college kids years ago, but Jeremiah's eyes were soft brown, big as saucers, and when he turned them on you, you just melted away and did what he wanted. Well, this here Joe and Jeremiah wandered all over the woods out there; the new super highway was planned but it hadn't gotten out to Joe's place, leastwise 'bout this time.

Well, Joe had a hobby. Seems like a long time ago, some one of his friends—or was it the scoutmaster—anyway, someone turned him on to photography. The first time Joe saw a roll of negatives come up all developed and pretty like, he just got hooked. Was worse, too, when he learnt how to make prints. Ole Joe never did get tired of watching them prints come up in the developer. Anyway, it seems that one day he read about how easy it was to make color prints and he decided he'd try it. He talked it over with Jeremiah (you see, Jeremiah loved to be in the darkroom with Joe, the light was soft and kinda reddish and ole Joe'd talk about how the print was coming up and all), so Jeremiah put up his head, and Jeremiah, he nodded his head, and old Joe, he filled out the coupon and sure enough! He got all the information and ordered the chemicals and paper and color film, and pretty soon ole Joe was developing his color negative film and making color prints.

Now ole Joe's photography was of the farm animals and some of the wild forest animals he made friends with and fed. In the winter when the snows came, most of the deer thereabouts knew old Joe was good for a handout and they'd just naturally meander up to the back door. So Joe, he took pictures of them, some head views, and sometimes he took pictures of the whole family. Joe was real proud of one of his pictures of the big buck and doe, and they'd brought the fawns along one spring and posed for a picture. In the spring, Joe liked to walk the fields and photograph the budding flowers and so many things in nature. He'd even bought a Macro-Zoom and pictured some grasshoppers on the sunflowers, and he had bees and butterflies on all sorts of flowers.

Well, about this time people began to admire his work. The folks around the county seat thought he had a real touch. You see, Joe didn't really know how to "balance" his color, but he used to remember how the fields looked on a summer afternoon with the golden glow that fell on the wheat, turning every blade of grass, every shaft of wheat into golden yellow treasures, and he'd try for that color. So he sold his work, and people paid well, but Joe kinda didn't charge too much, he liked to see them folks happy with his pictures. Finally, the farm work dwindled down and Joe found himself fast becoming a professional photographer. He decided he'd turn his hobby into money, seeing as how so many wanted them nature pictures of his.

Then ole Joe, he subscribed to all them photo-magazines and he done read everything he could to improve himself so's he'd be a real professional photographer.

Pretty soon, folks was telling him he oughta' join one of them "professional societies" and ole Joe found out the State Association of Professional Photographers met once a month up there at the State Capital, so ole Joe, one night when they was ameetin', he closed up the house and he and Jeremiah took off and he drove up there to the meeting. Well, turned out they didn't have any rules 'cepting he had to earn his living at photography and ole Joe, he was doing that anyway, so he joined, and he sat down with the rest of them professional photographers and they had some expert from out of state, he was telling them professionals how he made so much money and how he had a big studio with all them employees and how he had all kinds of honors, and Joe figured it must be true, 'cause he wore a ribbon 'round his neck.

Well, Joe went home after the meeting and he figured out how he'd change the old farmhouse into a studio and he'd do some portraits and charge them prices like that feller said and maybe get himself one of those ribbons. He talked it over with Jeremiah like he always did only this time, Jeremiah hadn't been with him up there to the meeting so Jeremiah didn't pay much attention. Time went on, Joe built a beautiful studio and folks came from all over the county seat to have their photographs taken by Joe. He changed his name to "Josiah, the Atelier," seems as how that was more fancy and fittin' for his new image and business was so good he had to hire a darkroom man and then a secretary. Ole Joe never was much good at letters and fancy writing so he had the secretary do it. They had new fancy darkrooms pretty soon and Jeremiah wasn't allowed in them— the darkroom man said Jeremiah just got in the way. Anyway, business flourished and Josiah (remember, that was his new name) attended all the meetings with those experts from out of state and he learned a lot. One of the first things was that he had to balance the prints, no more of that business of making prints over and over again until he got the feeling and mood he wanted. An expert up there at the state said he'd have to make a good print by the third try or his printing wouldn't pay off. Well, pretty soon,

Josiah learned how to advertise and his work was known all over the state and he had to hire some more people—he hired a photographer for the studio and another photographer to do the commercial work outside the studio and another darkroom assistant and even an office boy. The farm had changed some by now, Josiah had to get rid of the farm animals (wasn't good for the image) and he paved over the grass lawn for a parking lot and the state highway was built and the traffic meant he had a 100 percent location. His business prospered and he was even elected president of the State Association and became a delegate to the National Association. Pretty soon, Josiah had learned all the details of running a business, but he had to have a private office just so he could do the paperwork. Seems the federal government had almost a hundred forms he had to fill out and the advertising campaigns and his work with the other associations kept him at his desk until late evening. He never did get much of a chance to take pictures anymore, and he never got into the darkroom as this annoyed the darkroom man.

Well, anyway, a few years went on like this and one day Josiah stood outside the building and he reflected on his new life. He really had it made, as they say. He had this beautiful new modern contemporary studio made of stucco and cinder block with the new sculptured concrete driveway, all the new plastic evergreen shrubbery with the cedar chips for dirt and the fancy grass all over. Gone was the old Victorian farmhouse so lovingly crafted by his great grandfather and added onto by his grandfather and finally, his father had put on the side porch in the same style as the original; gone were the farm animals, his friends of just a few short years before, and even the deer didn't come around anymore for handouts, there was too much activity around the studio. Besides, they'd have never recognized the old place. And Jeremiah? Well, he died a few years back, probably because he wasn't wanted around the house, he got underfoot. And Josiah? Well, he never had time for those walks through the woods with Jeremiah, taking photographs of the flowers and the woodland animals; besides there wasn't room for such things anymore with the new highway and the traffic. He didn't get to take any photographs anymore either, since he was president of the company now and didn't have time; besides, that was the others' job now. He didn't even see the customers either, the receptionist delivered the photographs and so Josiah never did see the pleasure on clients' faces when they got their pictures. Yes, sir! Josiah was a real success now. You could tell.

He had all the honors a person could want—didn't even have to touch a camera, either! A real success, that's what he was, a real success.

# 14 The Photographer As an Artist

Ever since the invention of photography an argument has raged across this land as to whether or not photographs are "art." The controversy centers around the fact that the camera, without any help from the operator, functions so as to render anything in front of the lens as if it were drawn or painted. Its product is recognizable and does not need the ability to structure the image. The original complaint centers around this one characteristic of the camera. "Where is the artist?" they ask. *They,* in this case, are the painters, sculptors, musicians and writers who usually have dealt with "blanks": the writer, a blank piece of paper; the composer, another blank piece of paper; the sculptor, a few pounds of clay or a granite

91

block; and the painter, the pristine canvas. Invariably it required a great deal of talent, a modicum of training, and inspiration to bring forth on canvas, paper or granite, a recognizable image. On the other hand, because of its own ability to reproduce an image, the camera was thought to sidestep the creative process.

As photography grew—as a craft, if you will, or as a profession, if you have trouble accepting it as a craft—more and more photographers began to find ways to impress upon their photographs the "stamp" of their particular intentions. They began to manipulate images so as to create pictures that contained symbolism, such as Man Ray's photographs, which are stark, raw journalism; such as David Douglas Duncan's or W. Eugene Smith's work; or magnificent tonality in landscapes, such as the work of Ansel Adams. As more and more technical improvements were made in film and apparatus, more and more photographers found ways to stretch the literacy of photography and create images that were manifestations of their inner feelings. Yet competing with those photographers who tried desperately to control their techniques and wed them to their personal intellect were charlatans who capitalized on the "accident" of photography—that any photographer or *any* person, for that matter, with a modern automatic camera could expose film indiscriminately, in thousands of exposures, and could presumably obtain a handful of more or less exceptional photographs from the total number.

With today's photographic laboratories selling many skills that were part of the *craft* of all photographers before World War II (and still in the domain of the painter) and supplying enormous technical skills in the processing and finishing of prints, you begin to realize that the neophyte, by constant shooting and with the massive help of skilled people in the photographic laboratories, could, by the process of selection (which is, incidentally, an option not available to an artist in any other disipline), could conceivably come up with some great photographs.

What infuriates me and others is that often such a photographer's biggest asset is his or her "pushiness." For some unaccountable reason it seems that pushiness goes hand in hand with the charlatan, the same person who wins a merit at a PPofA show, has independent shows, publishes books, and is lauded by the critics. Not all, of course.

Fame is such a fleeting thing; the thirst and ambition of so many of us is the fuel that fires the boiler of our ambition.

The clear-thinking and intelligent photographer wishes to earn his laurels fairly and honestly in open competition with his peers. His less-principled brethren, on the other hand, win their laurels by any means available. What is unfortunate is that the very organizations that should be jealously guarding the gates of professional excellence have set and administered the rules and regulations so that they may be abused and misused for personal gain.

For twenty-five years I, as have others, have spoken out against certain judging practices, and especially one: the specific idea that a laboratory can make a print on the order of a photographer, who then submits this print to a jury for judging and eventually, the awarding of a merit point leading to a degree. This makes a mockery of the title Master of Photography.

It is now 25 years since I left active participation in the PPofA. (I am still a member and most likely will always be a member and support the organization.) Twenty-five years later, the view looks the same. It is inconceivable to me that a creative photographer could be awarded a merit based on a print made by a laboratory. Such an award says, in effect, that you do not believe that a print made by any laboratory and by a photographer in his or her darkroom would differ measurably. It says futher that the photograph was done at the moment of exposure. I cannot accept this, and I doubt that anyone who has ever worked in a creative darkroom believes that. The photographic process is total. Beside the consideration of the manipulation of light and the arrangement of objects, people or whatever the subject; of the selection of aperture and shutter speed; of the control and manipulation of exposure; the processing, development and printing of the image are part of a total process that does not end until the the creative darkroom techniques intended by the photographer have been completed. You may send all the work you wish to a laboratory in your day-to-day business operations, but when you ask to be judged for a national honor such as the Master of Photography, you should be the creator and the maker of your submission.

What is most disturbing is that so many galleries and museums are showing Gawdawful junk. Black and white, grainy, out-of-focus, poorly processed, with no real content, is being passed off as "photographic art" to an uninformed public. Most of this substandard work shows an enormous lack of skill, mostly in photographic technique, not to speak of the finishing.

Interestingly, most of these photographers are supported by grants from various foundations, including the National Endowment for the Arts. These foundations show a surprising lack of awareness in making their awards. The critics are no better. They are obsequious toadies prattling about "intellectual statements," filling column after column with intellectual drivel about the photographer's "inner soul." Not wishing to appear as Philistines, they laud this stuff with glowing comparisons to past greats, who, incidentally, weren't half as good as they're made out to be. The critics are impressed that the photographer has received a grant, and that the particular gallery, impressed with the grant, exhibits his work. So the critics write glowing reviews. And around and around we go.

Yet across this land there are hundreds and hundreds of very fine photographers with highly crafted and exquisitely finished work. Many of the PPofA Loan Collection Prints are truly works of art, but they bear the onus of being "commercial photographs" even though they are appreciated wherever they're exhibited. The photographers are not considered photographic artists by the New York clique. A shame, really. I wonder what history will honor: the casual dilettante with his grant and his pseudo-intellectual statement and his show of family album snapshots or some other inane subject chosen more with an eye toward the grant than toward producing a meaningful body of work; or "The Heartland of

America" that's close to the American flag, Apple Pie and Motherhood?

Most of this pretentious display has got to be one of the biggest put-ons in photographic art circles in this century. Some of the photographers' statements, neatly typed on small cards beneath the prints, are nothing more than intellectual garbage. I can't see why the profession sits still for it.

Almost every week I receive a poster, folder or brochure from a workshop showing black and white snapshot prints imitative of Cartier-Bresson but falling far short—prints you couldn't give away. Is this really is an example of "quality" work?

We need a reaffirmation of the standards and ethics of professional photography; we need a better understanding of what is commercial and what is art; we need to allow room for exploration; we need to recognize the need for photographic expression. But above all, we must be able to determine the difference between the serious experimenter and the opportunist.

# PART 2

# Professionalism

# 15 Marketing Your Photography

All the great photographs you've taken mean nothing as long as they sit in your files. If your purpose is to market your photography, you must learn as much about marketing as you did about many of the techniques of photography. Marketing your work is easy, very easy, but it's very precise and can't be left to chance or luck. You can't sit back and say you're above marketing, that selling your work is beneath you. If you don't feel enthusiastic about your own work, you won't be able to sell it. So, where does one start?

Assume you've taken many good 35mm transparencies and have made some better assemblages of them into new originals—since that's what they are,

99

new originals. These are essentially copies or copied on Ektachrome Duplicating Film 5071 as suggested by chapter 38, "The Importance of Duping." You should make at least 10 duplicates of each assemblage, thus creating at least 20 new images. This is your first goal. These 20 images are inserted into a plastic page after you have mounted them in *your* mounts. That's vital. You must not use Kodak mounts. You must buy and have imprinted *white,* not colored, mounts with your name, address and telephone number as well as the copyright symbol (©), the year in numerals and your name. Mounts can be purchased from the House of Marchese, 45 West 45th Street, New York, N.Y. 10036 (Pat Marchese). If you're not processing your own 5071, have it returned unmounted. It's less expensive and less likely to have scratches, and, of course, you won't have to break each mount open to reseal in your mounts. One of the marks of the professional is the mount. Besides, it provides your copyright.

Trim the three holes off the plastic slide page and it'll fit a Calumet #2 envelope or ship in a standard 9 × 12 envelope. I send a page of 20 35mm transparencies with a cover letter and a stamped, self-addressed envelope with each mailing. Do not fail to do all this. There is no need to send the slides by registered or certified mail, nor do you need a return receipt.

First you need three books that contain important addresses: *Photographer's Market* (Writer's Digest Books); *Photography Market Place* (R. R. Bowker Company); and *Stock Photo and Assignment Source Book* (R. R. Bowker Company). Make up a mailing list of all the major consumer magazines, making certain that the magazines you pick use illustration photography, all the greeting card companies, all the record companies and all the paper product companies. The paper product companies will have all the publishers of posters, calendars, notepads and all the stationery items that you see in the local discount store. This list will come to about 100 names, and it'll include some of the foreign companies, too. Try to get 20 classifications, since you want to send one set to each of the 20 companies. You made 10 sets, so you can only send 10 sets out the first mailing. As a set is returned, send it out *immediately* to the next name on the list. Be careful that you send each set to one *type* of company at a time—one greeting card company, one record production company, one book publisher, etc. You should sell one-time reproduction rights only, if and when a sale comes in. (See chapter 18, "Selling Your Rights.") A simple ring binder log of "In/Out" entries of the dates of the mailings and returns from prospects will keep things straight. I number each slide—no titles, no description. The bulk of the slides are filed in a Victor Slide File. If I need number 445, I go to the bulk file and flip through them numerically until I come to 445;, if they're all mailed, I mark that number down on a pad and next time I'm duping I make more.

This type of mailing serves many important purposes and is vital to your marketing plan. *You* pick and choose your clients. You mail to all the magazines, at the least, the top 20 consumer magazines. The art director sees your work over a period of a year; with a little bit of luck, you'll develop assignments and handle each one differently.

I shoot most assignments on 35mm, but I deliver

either 35mm or 4 × 5 or 8 × 10. The reason for the increased size has much to do with the creative image I'm making. For instance, I might have an assignment to illustrate a story in a woman's magazine pertaining to fear of falling. Fine, I might shoot two or three ideas, make my assemblages and deliver the 35mm. But if I wanted to overlay a "rippley" water texture screen, I make an 8 × 10 Ektachrome duplicate from the projected 35mm using the enlarger by overlaying the texture screen on the sheet of 8 × 10 film I've inserted in the easel over black backing paper. This imprints the screen. Since all positive copy material has one filter balance, I need only figure it once. Processing can be done by any lab; I do my own. Assignments pay about $750 for the photograph, $150 if you use models and $100 for processing. There's plenty of room for working slowly and carefully.

I start with this mailing of the 35mm slides, since that serves as a portfolio. No need to make up prints and trot around a city trying to see art directors; just mail your work. The only time I ever make a print is for one of two purposes; to exhibit at a lecture or one-person show or for teaching students. But I rarely have a print for sale. If one does sell then I have Berkey Custom Color labs in New York make a dye transfer, deliver it to the customer and bill me.

Even straight commercial studio photography is generated by this system. Often I'll mail to a specific advertising agency—one of the big ones I've found out about by checking the listings at the local library in the *Directory of Advertising Agencies,* and whose accounts I'm familiar with. I send the slides to the creative director, who, in turn, may either forward

them to a specific art director or give me an assignment himself. Once you have the account you may
very well have to use other cameras. I don't recommend doing food ads on 35mm. Still, you should refuse some jobs. I have all the facilities including all
the equipment I might need, but I still refuse jobs I
don't like, for a variety of reasons.

The letter accompanying the slides must spell
out in simple terms that you're enclosing a stamped,
self-addressed envelope and a list of slides; express
the hope that the director likes the work, say that he
or she is on a select list and will be solicited about
every three months. Don't go over one page double
spaced typing. Let the slides speak for themselves.
When a slide is purchased, you don't set the price—
the client does. The prices for greeting cards are
about $150, posters $250–$500, book jackets about
$300, and record covers are about $500.

# 16 Pricing Problems and Customs

Pricing is probably the most perplexing of all the business problems that photographers face, whatever their type of studio. A portrait photographer has specific ways of selling that differ from the commercial photographer, the photo-journalist, and the photo-illustrator. Most pricing practices are under the control of the photographer or his or her studio and normally should be evaluated on at least a annual basis although most companies have switched from annually to bi-annually—a situation something like a dog chasing its tail. Most photographic equipment and supply manufacturers regularly update their prices as soon as their raw material suppliers change theirs.

This round-robin tends to spiral upward at the rate of about 10 percent per year on any one item. Besides the prices of photographic equipment and supplies, living expenses increase at about the same rate. Add various taxes to this and you begin to feel the squeeze. It's not enough to say that you're not charging enough—you probably know that, but perhaps I can help you improve the basic structure of your pricing by giving you some guidelines—and by explaining some of the prevalent customs.

Let's get the prices that aren't under your control out of the way first. Photographers often ask prices to indicate solicitation photographs to greeting card, poster, record cover, playing card and consumer magazine clients. My answer is that you don't indicate a price at all, unless you simply won't sell at the prevailing rate. Each of the outlets will have fairly well established published rates. If you're interested in them and wish to have a booklet describing not only the various rates but also the type of rights, send to the American Society of Magazine Photographers (ASMP) for the *Pricing Portfolio.*

The 20 largest magazines pay approximately $600, plus models and lab fees for a single editorial use of a color photograph. Consequently, the payment is based on circulation and custom, and it has little to do with what the photographer may think his or her work is worth. If a photographer refuses such payment for a single photograph, the magazine can and will easily find plenty of others who are just as competent and who will jump to fill the assignment. So much for the established rates.

The portrait photographer has his customs, usually multiple pricing systems—one photograph, so much. Sometimes you see charges for sitting, retouching, coloring and all sorts of little extras. An increase in size brings more money, and even special finishes are variously charged.

I never could understand "proofs," so I never made any. (Of course we made them in the studio for ourselves.) After my customers got used to my way of doing business, they adapted and with nary a peep. I also abhorred the multiple pricing system. My thoughts were that if a photograph is worth, say, $35, then each duplicate photograph should be worth the same. I'm often reminded of the customer who, back in 1953, when told that one print was $35, two were $50 and three were $63, said he'd take one of the three for $21. And of course, he was right. No matter that I had a method of mass producing them and could make three cheaper than one. This multiple pricing system was esthetically hypocritical; on one hand I was trying to pass myself off as an artist, and on the other I was an assembly line manufacturer. Which are you, an artist or a manufacturer?

Commercial pricing had some peccadillos, too. For whatever reason, back in the early days, someone decided that 8 × 10 glossy reprints were or should be inexpensive; to this day, photographers are having trouble with 8 × 10 glossy reprint pricing. Most photographers lose money on reprints, but the real trouble with commercial pricing came with handling "time." This became a bothersome problem for the studio commercial photographer. One art director would set up a series of catalogue shots quickly and efficiently, the next would be a fuss-budget and nit-picker who would spend an hour playing with the product, so photographers soon had to add a "time" cost which translated into an hourly charge running parallel with the per picture price.

Location photography included the hourly rate but had to include also such expenses as mileage and props. So the commercial type price list developed all sorts of extra charges. I have pared the accompanying price list down to essentials. Two points are important: a price list should be dated and the commercial price list should not include either day-rate photography or illustration photography.

The day-rate price list should be self-explanatory, but again these price lists are subject to modification as your conditions change. The day rate is essentially the most dangerous one to use. Sometimes a client will want a day rate and then try to get either illustration or large format work done in the studio at that rate, intending to bypass the per picture price, which would cost him more. To the small town studio operator, a $600 day rate looks like avarice—believe me, it isn't. Most quality assignment photographers are getting even more. In fact, $1,300 a day is not uncommon for annual report photography. Remember, too, that these photographers don't have a studio nor do they use anything but a 35mm camera. *But,* they are truly experts and simply can't be stumped. Many times on such an assignment I've been asked to do a portrait of the president or the chairman. I shoot in 35mm and on Kodachrome II (I still have some!) with strobe lighting and have a dye transfer retouched 16 × 20 made. Frankly I consider it as good as any portrait done in a studio. This system, (transparency-dye transfer), incidentally, was the one used by the famous Bachrach Photographers for years, although they did use the 4 × 5 size for the transparencies.

The new E-6 films are finer grained and have a longer scale than their forebears, and the color saturation is more realistic—at the time of this writing, the films seem to have been improved and most of the problems with it are solved except, of course, the horrible temperature (105° F) needed, which makes it most difficult for the smaller photographer to control. These E-6 films hate air! This is one reason why most rotary-drum type processors had problems, and some still do. Oxidation is the anathema of all film or print processing, but the E-6 films are the most susceptible. Using these films on 35mm assignments is just now coming into favor and I heartily endorse them. The size of the film has nothing to do with the pricing. It's the image that really counts in our business, since the prices we charge are variable.

A studio type photographer called the other day with a problem in commercial pricing. I was astonished at his lack of understanding of this subject, and in checking my own group of students, I find all sorts of misconceptions. I hope this discussion will help those photographers who primarily do portraits and weddings but who are also doing some commercial work.

Pricing is relative. The actual amount of money you want for your work is probably the least important factor. The price of a photograph depends on your reputation, the competition, the economic situation of the country, the economic situation of your locality, what the client has been paying in the past, as well as other factors. The following are not factors: what you want, what you think you are worth, and your ability to perform. (These become factors in seeing the client for the second time.)

The first factor I mentioned was reputation. This usually does get a photographer his or her first job. He can even demand and get a high price if he can prove that such is his custom, but for the vast majority of photographers, pricing boils down to a procedure. If you have a strong reputation already, you don't need any help from me.

There are three basic forms of pricing. One is the "fixed" price for a specific job, say a product photograph for a brochure or catalogue. Another is the "multiple" pricing form where the first photograph is, say, $50; the second $35; and all thereafter, $30. This is a carryover from ancient portrait practices. The third is the "cost-plus." So much per photograph plus time plus expenses.

The fixed price is the photographer's way of saying, "It costs me so much to do business, with overhead, labor and cost of materials, plus a profit ratio of 20 percent." All of this is ludicrous to me, for it places the photographer in the position of being some sort of manufacturer on a "cost-plus" basis. If he sets a fixed price of, say, $50 and the client happened to fuss over each Polaroid photograph (at $1 each) for half a day, he'd soon change his pricing system.

As we have already seen, the "multiple system" has all of the problems of the "fixed" plus some of its own.

The "cost-plus system" is usually the best for one type of work: catalogue or brochure product photography without models. It works like this: all photographs are the same price; a 4 × 5 color transparency of any product would be $50. However, time is charged at the rate of $25 per hour along with the print or transparency price. Polaroid photographs are $1 apiece and props are charged for separately.

I used to use all of these at one time or another. Now I use a system that uses parts of all of the above. I don't tell clients this so please don't quote me. It is *what the traffic will bear:* I have different quotes for different folks. But—and this is a big but—I had to become well enough known before I could do it.

There is logic in what I am doing. I might do the cover for an advertising agency of one of their clients' catalogues, and it would require "creative color photography." That's why they came to me instead of using the local photographer. So I might ask for and get $250 and it might be, and usually is, just a 35mm transparency.

If the same single photograph is to be used in, say, *Life* and the page rate in *Life* on a one-time use basis was $60,000 and my photograph was the central theme, I'd be entitled to up to $1,000 or whatever I could get. I have done many *Life* and *Look* photographs that brought in only $500—that was all I could get. But let's be realistic. If I did the *Life* ad yesterday, and today a motel wants a Dexter postcard, I would charge $50, and, frankly, that's all I think it would be worth. If I were a beginner, I would charge $25, because that is just about the rock bottom for that type of job in this country in almost every area. But I could see parts of our country, say sections of the rural South, where a raw, starting photographer might have to ask $10 or face stiff competition!

The client will give you a hint! Suppose he or she comes to your studio—you do strictly portraits and weddings—and he or she asks for a commercial job. Right away, you know he doesn't have much knowledge about handling commercial photographers or he wouldn't be at your studio. Listen to what he wants. If he speaks with sure understanding, uses our vernacular, shows you tear sheets of things he has cut out of magazines—then you know what he wants. In looking at the samples he shows you, you know if you can do the job. If he shows you jobs taken by the world's greats at fantastic locations with models, run as fast as you can for the safety of your darkroom. *There is no way on earth that you can even come near to what he wants.* Even if he says, "Of course I realize it won't be this good, but . . . ." don't take the job! If you do, you are doomed to fail and may even have trouble collecting.

If he shows you last year's catalogue and says he is unhappy about it, do you have the knowledge to figure out if you are looking at a poor printing job or poor photography? If either of these is the case, doesn't that suggest to you that he doesn't know what he is doing? Why did he buy a poor printing job or a poor photographer? Ask to do a sample. Estimate your price, give him a fixed price on one photo, do it and ask if he is satisfied with the price and the photo. Then go into the contract for the rest of the job.

Another thing: unless you have a great deal of experience or have attended a school or many workshops, about all you are going to do is "light, focus and expose." That is the simplest form of photography. You throw light around or tent hell out of the product or use direct or umbrella and wind up with a well exposed transparency, thanks to Kodak, Sinar, and your meter. What comes out is a sharp, colorful reproduction of his product. He, being as ignorant as you, accepts the job. The poor printer prints it and another piece of you-know-what-I-mean is published.

*There is a great difference between a product shot and an illustration,* and that directly influences pricing. Take the technical knowledge first. A tent is not a cureall. A tent adds white to every color in the photograph, so that reds become pink, green becomes light green, blue becomes powder blue. If the color of the product is a *Trademark* color, you can't tent.

Are you aware that every field of view (the area taken in by the camera) under two feet requires a great deal of knowledge of bellows and reciprocity problems? Did you know that every field of view over two or three feet (leaving the table top) requires a great deal of knowledge about lighting, but no problems of bellows draw exposure and reciprocity? Do you know how to "fine-filter?" This is one of the areas where the super-pro leaves the beginner.

Can you look at the client's products and know instantly what your problems are going to be? Don't you think you should know? And if you do know all this, don't you think you should be paid for it? Do you know how to describe these problems to the client? Do you have the equipment to do the job or are you going to bluff your way through and then complain because you have a hard time collecting for such a job?

Think and listen, and find out everything you can before you accept the job. Make sure the client understands, before you begin, what the whole naked cost will be.

God made light, and the light made a shadow where something interfered. The difference between the highest highlight visible to the naked eye and the deepest shadow visible is a ratio of 100,000:1. Just as soon as you snap the shutter, you compress that ratio to 1000:1, because the lens opening was fixed at a certain f stop, whereas your eye adjusts rapidly when you look from highlight to shadow, closing down in the sunlight and opening up in the shadow. Elementary, right?

The sun is 93 million miles away, so if you picture two people 10 feet apart outdoors, there is no need to light the person farther from the lens. The ratio between 93 million miles and 10 feet is surprisingly negligible in this situation. Let's go inside now. You turn on the light. Wow! All 1,000 watts! If the distance between the light and the first subject is 10 feet and the second subject is 10 feet farther, you need a two-stop increase in exposure to compensate. Yet outside you had the same conditions except for the light. You brought the light much closer and light, all light, the sun included, follows the inverse-ratio law. Your meter will prove it to you.

Back to our contrast ratio for a moment. On the film, you have compressed the ratio to 1000:1; you show that transparency to the art director or client and he, being uninformed, says, "Wow." Only you just screwed him—and yourself out of the next job, because a transparency, by the very nature of viewing something by transmitted light, allows you to look into the shadows; your eye will adjust and see detail that is in the transparency. Conversely, your eye will close down to let you look at detail in the highlights. *But* when this is printed on anything, the contrast ratio is once again compressed to about 100:1. You have taken away the *translucence,* so the eye now looks at the color-printed page and can stick to one f stop.

What has happened? What has happened to the other details? They were dropped out at the camera exposure, but by using the median exposure you retained the *essentials* or perhaps I should say you abstracted the scene. When your transparency was printed on the page, the printer lost all sorts of highlights and shadow detail because he used *opaque* ink. Everyone is disappointed in the final result. You don't get the next job, someone else who really knows how gets the job. Price? No object as long as it is reasonable. Success breeds success, and the key to all success is knowledge.

When you are using color films, *compress the ratio before you shoot!* You do that by softening all outdoor light with scrims, flats, shades, shower glass curtains or what have you. If you can't knock down the light, fill in the shadows. You do this until your meter says 3-1, highlight to shadow. And remember this, too: *filling with light isn't the same as softening the main.* No way!

Now let's go inside to a small product. You turn a light on the product. Then fill it in so that the ratio from highlight to shadow is 3-1. *Don't shoot!* That's a terrible picture. True, you retained the detail and the printer can print, but the picture is esthetically poor. Raw light isn't the light to use. What you need is *very high intensity* softened with shower curtain material and coming from a direction that should show texture, usually from behind the product, or side lighting. Fill to what you need, and the fill light must also be soft. *Don't trust your eyes!* Eyes love to look into shadows and highlights; if you're using a view camera, shoot a Polaroid. If you are using a smaller format, be ever aware of the trickery of your adjustable iris diaphragm eyeball!

What happens next? If your transparency has compressed the ratio and you have shown the art director or client how it will look on paper, you have eliminated 90 percent of the pricing problem. Some very good rules:

1. Use the highest intensity of light you can, but soften it.
2. Use an excellent meter with incident and reflected light readings.
3. Compress the ratio between highlight and shadow to 3:1.
4. Show the client something backed up with paper, preferably a Polaroid.
5. Use only back or side for the main light, and fill from the front.
6. When in doubt, use the softest lighting available, and the color will act as the contrast.
7. If you are still unsure, go to the idiot's light, umbrella strobe.

# 17 Protect Yourself

Needing a copyright on a photograph hasn't been much of a bother to the average photographer; after all, who needs some of the photographs you're *required* to take? Most commercial jobs, some ads, and almost all portraits seem to fall into this category. The real reason for needing a copyright is to protect a photograph that can be sold again and again, in which case you'd need to own the rights—all rights. In the past, applying for a copyright was a bit tedious and somewhat costly. You had to fill out form "J" and send six dollars with each request. Some of us who were closer to the problem soon discovered that we could photograph a sheet of slides and copyright the entire sheet of 20 for the same six dollars. But this, too, was expensive and tiresome—many photographers gave up. Some photographers had to apply for copyrights because of other problems. Often their work was plagiarized. Slides were copied by greeting card companies and sometimes by stock houses, and, occasionally, you would find your work used without payment. In one or two cases where I found my work copied and used, it wasn't worth suing over since the time and costs for trials and attorneys were far greater than I would get as an award if I won the suit.

All of this has changed rather dramatically with the Copyright Act of 1976, which took effect on January 1, 1978. Under the old law, you had to prove you had copyrighted something; under the new law the photographer owns the copyright unless he or she signs away these rights. If you are the creator of any work as a photographer, it is copyrighted at the moment of creation, and if you label it "Copyright 1978 John Jones," you're protected—even without filing a copyright. No need to wait until it is published.

The old copyright provided protection for a term of 28 years and had to be renewed at the end of that time or the work fell into the "public domain," which means anyone can use it without payment to you. Under the new law the term has been extended to the life of the creator (read photographer) plus 50 years. Your heirs could have an income from your copyrighted material.

There are two terms you should be familiar with. One written in the new law speaks of a work commissioned by a client as "work made for hire." This phrase, if used by your client and appearing on a written document such as a letter of assignment or a purchase order, means the client will own the copyright, unless, of course, you can persuade the client to sign an agreement giving you the rights you want. What most of us ask for is to own those photographs taken on the assignment but not used by the client. The other term defines "work for hire" as "a work specially ordered or commissioned for use as a contribution to a collective work." Here too, the client owns the copyright. If you see either of these statements, be wary—unless you're prepared to give away all rights, don't sign the agreement.

The *General Guide to the Copyright Act of 1976* can be obtained from the Copyright Office, Library of Congress, Washington, D.C. 20559. Their definition of a "work made for hire," is ". . . a work prepared by an employee within the scope of his employment." If you fit this definition, the client owns the work.

This copyright business is easily understood. Most of it is a matter of communication with the client. Difficulties can be avoided by spelling out what terms you're working under. Most small commercial photographers don't get a purchase order in the mail—more likely, the client phones and says something about coming over and shooting some photos. Chances are that kind of work isn't something that would have another market anyway, but if it should, and you wish to resell—you're going to have to answer such a call with a letter of acceptance spelling out the terms and *signed* by you. To make it legal, you're going to have to ask the client to sign it, too. This mumbo jumbo is not really necessary in most cases. Incidentally, advertisements are not considered "work for hire." When you photograph something for an ad, you own the subsidiary rights and the copyright.

My experience with professional photographers indicates that most of them are sloppy when they make up invoices. I've seen some terrible phraseology used. If you want to protect yourself, you're going to have to spell out the rights and something we've never had to do before—you must *sign the invoice.* Incidentally, if you sue and win, you can now collect the legal fees, or rather sue for them in the same case. Just don't lose. This means attorneys who heretofore avoided this type of case like the plague are now going to clamor to represent you. Just make sure you're on firm ground.

Signing the invoice, submitting an acceptance of assignment letter, using the proper terms for the releasing of rights (see my book, *Photography for the Professionals*) are all fine, but there's one more thing to do: stamp or imprint your photography with the copyright symbol, the year and your name. My suggestion to any photographer—portrait, commercial or journalist—is to rubber stamp the back of all prints with this legend and where possible to affix the symbol, date and name to the face of the print and certainly on all transparency mounts. Incidentally, use only cardboard mounts—they have to be torn apart to get rid of the symbol. Even mark your forms, such as the finishing envelopes, file envelopes, anything and everything, although you might not file with the Copyright Office. This method is sufficient and legally arguable. Of course transparencies that are to be sold over and over again (a method I teach in the Creative Color Workshops) should be filed for a copyright in groups of 20 slides.

Be ever wary of using the word *sell* unless it is

accompanied by the word *rights.* Otherwise you could be in trouble. Try *lease* or perhaps *rent.* You might ask for credit when your photograph is published. Also ask for the copyright symbol and date to appear with your name, and *don't forget to ask for your original transparency back.*

I caution photographers who aren't in the business of selling reproduction rights not to confuse their clients with some of this legal terminology—it tends to scare off those who are uninformed. The people we deal with, mostly magazine and book publishers, are knowledgeable and well aware of the new Copyright Act, so when they see photographs with copyright restrictions, they understand. Surprisingly, even a school portrait is now copyrightable, although I can't see what the point is, since to resell a portrait would get the photographer in legal trouble because of "invasion of privacy." Portrait photographers plagued by photo store copying can stop the practice by placing the copyright symbol on all prints and proofs. Those of you making photographs of models (the human kind) must still adhere to the model release, and you must not resell photographs without permission. Incidentally, if you plan to sell more than once, the model release must say so. You can't hire a model to pose with, say, an office machine, have him or her sign a model release, and then use an outtake from the shooting for another purpose—he or she can sue and collect. I word my releases to be all inclusive by stipulating that I own all reproduction rights, now or in the future. Of course, these models are usually local rather than from the large model agencies.

The new Copyright Act is a Godsend to assign-

ment photographers. Much credit for the ground-
work belongs to organizations such as The Authors
Guild, The American Society of Journalists and Authors, and The American Society of Magazine Photographers.

# 18 Selling Your Rights

I've had a number of fundamental principles regarding how I conduct myself as a professional photographer for the last 12 years. These rules guide me in the day-to-day dealings with clients. A photographer should not sell all rights to his photographs; a photographer should sell each photograph over and over again until the market is saturated with each one. A photographer should never sell the "original." (In my case, this is easy, since there isn't any such thing; all my photographs contain more than one image; therefore, which copy/duplicate is the original? Frankly, I consider them all to be originals.)

I also believe in flexible pricing, or what the traffic will bear, as opposed to printed price lists. I believe that the camera and the other photographic apparatus and equipment are just tools to be treated well and used properly but not worshipped as if they had some Godlike power. I believe a professional photographer has a mandate with his soul to learn his photographic techniques, to become a craftsman as quickly as possible and then to recognize that his mind is the greatest creative tool in his life. I believe that to be a great photographer you must be a life-long student of the liberal arts. I believe the photograph is *never* completed at the moment of exposure and that an integral part of the creative process of a photograph is the darkroom technique.

This means a change in attitude from our present position that the camera single exposure is the complete product. Today it is necessary for photographers to realize that photographs can be marketed over and over again. Of course this does not apply to the portrait and commercial subjects produced by the average photographic studio. Those are photographic documents that quite properly have value only to the subject or corporation that commissioned them. I visualize the professional photographer as one who makes a wide variety of photographic images of his own choosing and markets these without regard to establishing a place of business called a studio, without specified hours, without being open to the public, without being a valet to the whim of unknowing customers who reduce his art to the lowest level, without grovelling before the almighty dollar. Such idealism is most commendable but highly impractical to maintain in today's economy.

Now to the Rights. This is probably one of the important areas in the *business* of photography. The semantics of selling require that we all understand what is meant by *rights. Reproduction rights* is the base of this subject, so the individual headings assume "reproduction." The most onerous entry is *all rights,* which means not only reproduction but custody. The term requires little explanation, since it means exactly what it says: All rights are sold. This phrase is used where you are working for a product or service and can't resell the photograph to anyone else anyway—and wouldn't want to. Most large advertising campaigns are sold this way and such things as catalogues. Flyers and sales literature for products also fall into the all-rights category, not to mention general run-of-the-mill commercial and most portrait photography. *All rights* is very similar to *Exclusive rights,* except that with the latter you could add another word that would clearly define what you are selling. Think of *Exclusive GREETING CARD rights.* The words "greeting card" amplify "exclusive." You could then use words like "record cover," "poster," "jig-saw puzzle," "textbook," "encyclopedia," and so on. As to pricing, both *all rights* and *exclusive* should obviously command the most money.

World rights defines the geographic limits. With the world getting smaller every day, more and more photographers are soliciting worldwide, so *world rights* also needs a secondary word for amplification. Just use the same words as above, i.e., "greeting cards," etc. So your billing might read: *"world playing card rights"* or *"North American poster rights"; "European textbook rights";* one I use quite often is *"foreign language rights."*

Sometimes you need further amplification and I

use a tertiary phrase such as *one time. One time* can be placed in front or in the middle or added at the end of the phrase. *One-time world poster rights* pins down the use. *One-time reproduction jig-saw puzzle rights* might be another. *One-time North American greeting card rights* is still another phrase. The ASMP suggests an even further delineation such as "language." They might have: *one-time rights in two languages.*

Whatever the phrasing, the purpose is to define clearly what you are selling. Most problems with clients arise from a lack of communication. The clearer you can be the better, but—a big but—don't aggrandize your work. I've seen photographers' invoices that looked like an IBM contract—all for a $20 picture of an oil delivery truck. Common sense dictates that you use good judgment and don't overestimate your own importance or the value of your work. Many photographers show me "pretty picture" slides of flowers and tell me that they're making mailings to such and such a magazine, agency or whatever—it's an exercise in futility. If I say something about the ordinary or common quality of the slide they think it professional jealousy. Your work has to be good. Who makes that judgment? I really don't know. I use demonstrated sales as my criterion as well as an enormous amount of reading and looking at published greeting cards, record covers, editorial illustrations, advertisements, packaging, puzzles, textbooks, and encyclopedias.

You should write on your invoice that you expect the purchased transparency to be returned, that it is your property and has a value. In some cases, you will have to be the judge; I suggest stating an arbitrary value. If you send duplicate-originals, as I do, never let the client know he has a copy or dupe. As far as your client is concerned he has the original.

If you have recognizable models in the photograph, be careful to have a model release. Most magazines will require either a photocopy or the original—especially when they're billed for their appearance.

Keep a list of the sales for each photograph, and if there is any overlapping be sure to warn the client. Some clients, most, in fact, like to hear that a photograph they picked has also been used in another media. Conversely, some don't like it at all. Write down the type of *right* you released on the file card.

Sometimes I write "Subsidiary rights retained" —this is further amplification, or perhaps I should say clarification, since the retention of additional rights is implied when the invoice reads *one-time North American reproduction rights released.*

Another caution. Much of this is nonsense when dealing with local clients and would only tend to muddy communications between you, so be careful, and don't be in too much of a hurry to formalize your invoices in the vague hope that fancy talk will make you more of a professional. To me, a warm handshake is still worth more than all the contracts in the world. I'd much rather have a *personal* relationship with my art director or advertising manager. I work for a number of magazines this way. I wouldn't want to ask for a purchase order, and when I submit my invoice, I don't clutter it up with a lot of phoney gobbledegook. Yet I do use this formal phraseology, mostly with strangers and some clients, but sometimes I think this "rights" business is overdone. I do know one field in which I do use all the phrases and that's book publishing, most especially textbook and encyclopedia publishing. They're used to dealing in such contractual terms, and you need the protection.

When I sell abroad, I tell my clients where else I have sold a particular photograph, to prevent over-lapping. I also mention just which rights have been sold and which are still available. If I feel there might be a conflict, I don't send that transparency.

# 19 What's a Right, and What Isn't

You're out in the park and you see a cute child playing on a swing and you make an exciting shot with blurred motion, but since you used a flash with the slow shutter speed the child is "stopped" at the end of the action and is, therefore, recognizable. Back at the studio or your office after processing, you realize you have the makings of a good illustration, but you have neither a model release nor a chance of getting one. What are your rights and what are not?

If you sell this picture as a greeting card, poster, record cover, or illustration for an editorial or article, you don't need a release. But you can't sell it as an illustration for a brochure that advertises a product or an advertisement where the illustration is used alone or with other photographs and might suggest endorsement by the person photographed.

The trick here is "invasion of privacy." No matter what you use the photograph for, it would be illegal if you took the photograph on private property, especially that of the home of the child or even outside on the lawn or backyard. That would be trespass. Since you took the photograph in a public place, in this case a park, you aren't invading the child's privacy. However, there are exceptions. Once in a while someone does something in public but attempts to hide the action; perhaps your camera caught the child doing something that would prove embarrassing to the child or the child's parents. Think of, say, wind blowing a dress in such a way that would expose underwear. To make that photograph and sell it would be an outright violation of invasion of privacy concepts.

You can't alter the photograph either, at least not in any way that would be embarrassing to the subject. You can alter it in many other ways that would make the photograph more acceptable for publication, though, such as adding a blurred flower overlay that would effectively disguise the features of the person. But any alteration that suggests or implies a characteristic that is not true is considered an invasion of privacy; for instance, adding an overlay of a nude to your photograph of the child.

The point is that invasion of privacy doesn't mean invading the geographic limits of the subject. Invasion of privacy is the invasion of the rights of the individual. Think of it as objectionable publicity. If your photograph fits that category, the chances are that you have, in fact, invaded the subject's privacy.

Furthermore, you cannot be the judge of objectionable publicity; only the subject can determine that.

If you are taking photographs *for your own use* and in a public place, go ahead, since invasion of privacy generally refers to having the picture published. If you use the photograph just for your own enjoyment, no harm done.

But we are professionals, and our game is marketing, so we must have guidelines to go by. It's quite easy to say, "When in doubt have a signed model release." But you can't always get one and you don't always need one. Most of this business of model releases is based on common sense anyway, but remember that anyone can sue anyone whether or not they have a case. Because of the nuisance and bother of suits it's best to be overcautious. So get one if you can.

Model releases aren't a guarantee of compliance with the law. It's entirely possible to sign a contract, have it notarized and assume you are operating legally when, in fact, you may have violated the law in the contractual agreement. You simply can't "contract" away or circumvent an existing law. So the palaver about a "legally written" model release is sheer nonsense. If you've invaded the privacy of a subject and published a the photograph, you can still be sued and, moreover, lose the suit. Much has to do with common sense, as I've mentioned. The law is also concerned with "intent." A model who sues you for publishing a photograph of him or her in a greeting card—a "love" card—would have a hard time proving that you damaged his or her reputation in some way. However, if you are sued because you photographed a model with the intent to defraud him or her by using the photographs for your own purposes without payment of the model's usual fee (the model would have to prove by receipts that what he or she sued for is the usual fee), then the model could probably collect.

I find that it's best to alter the photograph with the addition of an overlay of diffusion, colored balls of light, and out of focus, colored feathers or flowers. But these devices are unnecessary in most cases since I generally sell to magazines, greeting cards, record covers, book jackets and the like where I don't often have the problem. Of course, when I am being paid on an assignment, I do have the model sign a release and I do pay her. This is quite obvious. My comments concern those cases where you have taken "grab" shots and later found a market for them.

When I hire models, who are local friends rather than professionals, I do pay them and ask for a release. Even a signed release and payment of only one dollar can suggest to the model that he or she doesn't have any legal recourse, but again, this assumes your use of the photograph doesn't constitute an invasion of privacy and that you have not defaced or so altered the photograph so as to embarrass him or her. Probably the biggest problem is with lighting, taking and selling of nude photographs. Sexual attitudes aside, most photographers love to take nudes. They represent the ultimate challenge to the photographer. A good nude photograph is an expression of high quality artistry in photography. Anyone who has tried making them knows just how difficult they are. If you feel such photographs might embarrass you or the subject, just make your photographs so that the face doesn't show. This is one area where you should be sure to have a signed model release.

Can one release cover more than one use? Yes, mine do. I rarely let the model think that the release applies to only one use. After all, the model has the right to refuse to work. A few years ago, a man and woman posed for me nude because they needed the money desperately. I paid them $100 and took some five or six rolls of 120 transparency material. I'm still selling photographs from that session, and the models will be grandparents before I finish. It has always been my policy to own my own photographs and sell them over and over again.

When you hire a model from an agency, the implication is that the photographs are to be used for the one original purpose and that the release does not include other uses. Be careful when you hire a model from a reputable model agency. I have taken Black Velvet whisky, Smirnoff vodka, Don Q rum and many cigarette ads using women and men from agencies such as Ford and Wilhelmina in New York. I would not use those transparencies for any purpose other than the one I hired the models for without requesting permission, which would most likely result in a request for an additional fee. And quite rightly so. As a matter of fact, just recently, I have noticed a change in model agency practices. They have asked for additional fees, calling them "residuals," for point of purchase published photographs used beyond six months. This change is most probably the result of television's practice of paying residuals when a show is rerun, which brings up a very interesting point. Should we, as illustrative photographers, be paid when our photographs are used more than once or are published in more than one medium? Those of us in the ASMP have long recognized the need to be paid *for each use,* but it's easier said than done in practice. We're delighted to have the job and rarely do we make waves with the client at the time of the contract. Arrogant photographers have little clout and would do great service to themselves if they didn't demand purchase orders and stopped setting all sorts of conditions on their photography.*

*I must place a disclaimer here: This chapter is based on my own opinions, understanding and experience and is not necessarily legally definitive, nor should it be used as such. I write it thus in the hope that I might clear some muddied waters and prove useful to others.

# 20 The Photographer As Publisher

At one time or another, every photographer has thought of publishing a book of his or her photographs. Over the years many of your friends have admired your work and perhaps one among them has even suggested publishing a book. In many ways it's not such a bad idea, yet it's not as easy as one might think. Some 40,000 individual titles are published each year in the United States, but the average person hears only of a few hundred at most. The media give reams of coverage to sensations such as Mario Puzo's *Fools Die* when the combination paperback and movie rights sell for $2,500,000. And there's the chance that some scribbler in northern Vermont may write about the early West and the novel may become a best seller. That's the dream that makes all authors sit up and pay attention—the hope of every scribbler.

Photographers read about these fortunate people and think that they might have a head start. After all, they can put out a book of photographs with little text other than captions. But it's really not that easy. Publishers are a wary breed, given neither to charity nor to believing in making a contribution to the arts in America. They're profit oriented, as they should be if they're responsive to their stockholders. A book must sell. More important, it must sell without much advertising. Your book, no matter how great the photographs, is doomed before it's printed unless you're well known, and not just in the photographic community. If you've had one-man shows in galleries, if your work has appeared in consumer magazines and if you've received recognition from the photographic critics, you have a formidable start, but publishing your book still won't be easy.

This isn't to say you couldn't publish a book yourself. If you do, you'll be in some excellent company. Many famous authors have "dabbled" in self-publishing. But "vanity publishing" is something to stay away from. What's the difference between "trade," "self," and "vanity?" Trade publishers are houses that make a business of selling books to bookstores, libraries, book clubs and through direct mail. They assume the costs of producing the book and publishing it. They often have to put out about 100 or more titles a year, each year, in order to keep their heads above water. They have to maintain sales forces all over the country to call on bookstores. They have to maintain warehouses with computer facilities for billing, shipping, credit and collection—this is called fulfillment. The office staff of editors, editorial assistants and general personnel handle the contacts with book clubs, paperback publishers, special sales and, of course, the handling of the manuscripts and authors.

So-called vanity publishers generally charge the author for these and other services rendered in handling the book. "Self-publishing" involves the author's actually becoming the publisher—creating and marketing his own work.

Manufacturing books follows precise formulas. As one prime example, the printing bill including the dust jacket of any proposed book should not exceed one-sixth of the list price of the book. Let's break down the figures for a moment: let's say a book is proposed to sell at $10, which is doubtful in today's economy; anyway, 40 percent, or $4, is the average discount to the local bookstore. That's the heftiest discount in the process. Astonishingly, a bookstore can return unsold books for *full discount* and at any time up to a year after publication. Easily the most liberal business arrangement you could imagine. This one characteristic governs many other facets of the book publishing business and is one reason why royalties are paid on six months' basis for sales made as much as nine months earlier. And furthermore, the sales would not count until the actual bill is paid, so as much as a year and even more could conceivably go by before the author would get his or her royalty.

Now we have $6 left. 10 percent of that, or 60 cents, goes to the sales person; 25 percent of the $6, or $1.50 goes for fulfillment. Some publishers don't own their own warehouses and fulfillment facilities and use specialists like Baker and Taylor, Brodart and Ingram. So now out of our $10 list price we've spent $4 for the bookstore, $1.50 for fulfillment, 60 cents for the sales person and 10 percent or $1, for the author. What do we have left? A big fat $2.80. Now for the printing bill. Remember I said we must not pay more than one-sixth of the list price for printing, jackets and binding, so to round off some figures, let's use 17 percent, or $1.70, for the cost of printing the book. To get that figure nowadays, you'd have to print a book with no illustrations, and the absolute minimum number of copies would be 10,000. Binding alone costs around 60 cents for each book, with a cloth (hard cover) cover, including dyes and stamping.

Now the publisher has $1.10 left for publicity, advertising and promotion and that thing called the bottom line—the profit. Sounds grim.

Well, it isn't all bad. For instance, libraries get only a 20 percent discount, book club sales are split 50-50 with the author, foreign and other subsidiary sales are also split with the author, and sometimes the book takes off and you go back for second, third and more printings. This time your cost of printing goes down because the typography, design and most of the up-front expenses are already paid.

But what if your book contains photographs? Black and white photographs mean costs for plates. This runs the cost of the book printing way up, which runs the list price up accordingly, in order to stay within the formula. And God forbid you should decide you want a book of *color* photography. Plates made in the United States are very expensive. Even contracting the work in Japan or in Italy, which was the usual practice before the reevaluation of the yen, and lira, has become exhorbitantly expensive. The minimum number of copies in a printing is 12,500 and the cost with, say, some 50 plates in full color will be around $4 a book. This means that the book must list for $24, a price that most likely will affect sales adversely. Also, the publisher would have to put up $50,000 instead of $17,000 for a book without illustrations.

Add to this the demands of some authors for enormous advances against royalties, and you can begin to see some of the problems publishers have. If you self-publish, you have all of the problems above plus hundreds of dollars spent in spinning your wheels, simply because you don't have the expertise to be efficient. But the main problem of doing your own publishing is that you don't have a way of distributing the books after you do find your way through the maze of production. The major distributors are high-volume houses and simply wouldn't be interested in a one-book publisher no matter how well it might sell.

If you do decide to publish yourself, you must come up with somewhere in the neighborhood of $25,000. And you can expect to spend an enormous amount of time learning new skills. The chances of financial success are quite slim. One way you can tell if you have the book that could sell is to present your proposal to the regular trade publishers. If they want the book—that's your indication that you have a saleable book. The most profitable way for you to sell your book is by direct mail; that is, taking ads in various journals, photographic and otherwise, selling at the full list price plus shipping and handling.

The cost of advertising is horrendous and any publisher will tell you that advertising alone will *not* sell books, especially "picture" books or "coffee table" books.

The best way to get published and make money is to do what you know best—photography—and let the publishers buy your book and pay you a royalty on copies sold.

# 21 Managing Your Money

Managing money is a life-long task. When we were youngsters, it was quite simple: if we were lucky, we got an allowance; if we were even more fortunate, we earned our allowance by doing odd jobs, and the luckiest break of all, at least to me, was being brought up by my grandfather, a frugal Scotsman, who, although he was one of the wealthiest men in New York, insisted that not only must I earn my allowance, but the tasks must be legitimate—not "clean up your plate" or "straighten out your room." Oh no, you were expected to do those things. His idea was that I should find odd jobs to do outside the family. True, he directed my efforts and acted as my financial advisor, but he never interfered or interceded when I made a

poor deal or my zeal clouded my thinking and I con-
tracted for work that was a waste of time for the
money involved.

One of my first jobs was as a *Collier's* magazine
subscription salesman. At that time, in 1930 in New
York City, *Collier's* used young boys and some girls as
salespeople. The rewards were quite startling. This
was how I earned my first Columbia two-wheeler.
Another job was walking the pedigreed dogs of the
wealthy families on our block, a block of townhouses
and also of speakeasies. I soon graduated to holding
umbrellas over elegantly dressed flappers and their
dandies as they alighted from their limousines and
taxicabs on rainy nights. The tips were good; a dime,
15 cents and sometimes a two-bit piece. Two dollars
for an evening was not uncommon. And remember,
this was during the days when a good salary was
twelve dollars a week!

My mother was scandalized; walking the dogs of
her society friends was one thing, selling magazine
subscriptions was, well, kind of cute, but opening
doors and holding your hand out for a tip—wasn't
that too common? My grandfather felt that working
for unpromised money was good for me. He was so
right! He felt I might learn some respect for money;
more important, I learned respect for the working
classes of my day. The point was, I was learning to be
independent, I was learning to depend on myself and
my own efforts and not to expect that, being the
grandson of a wealthy publisher (Forbes Publishing
Company), I would never need to earn a living. He
was right again, especially since I didn't inherit a
nickel!

I learned some other lessons as a youngster; I

learned the value of being a *commission sales person* as opposed to being salaried. I've never forgotten that I can and do earn more, and have earned more for the last forty years than I could have as a salaried person. With the exception of two years with the Eastman Kodak Company, I've never formally worked for a salary.

It takes a certain kind of guts to hustle on your own, and it takes a certain kind of character to be able to accept the frustrating uncertainty of solicitation. Those that thrive on it are usually outgoing and extroverted personalities with a great deal of self-confidence. If they're fortunate enough to have a good education as well, they're hard to beat. They're the captains of industry, statespeople and political leaders, leading scientists, research chemists, and the curious intellectuals that populate our literature and our philosophy.

Those without formal education are usually self-taught. Look out for them! They're fine people, just intense and determined, and their personalities reflect their enormous urge to succeed. They usually do. In commission circles, these are the types that exceed their quotas. This breed needs no overseer, no boss, no sales manager—they're self-starters and they're able to drive themselves unbelievably—more than any boss could or would.

The lower strata of these are the charlatans, the confidence men and women, the type about whom a penologist would say, "If he'd only use his talents for honest work, he'd go to the top." I think that writers fall into this last category, too. After all, they get paid for putting down on paper wild stories and fantasies that in any other profession would merit their being labeled a liar. So managing money successfully starts in childhood but can be learned at any age. Right now photographers are in a buyer's market; by that, I mean that the competition for the camera dollar is so great that anyone who pays over 10 percent above dealer net for photographic equipment or supplies is simply wasting money. How long this "buyer's market" will last is hard to predict. Japan is in an economic depression; Europe finds the price of the mark and the pound exceeding the value of the dollar—translated, that means something you buy this year will cost you more next year.

The average photographer should take a lesson from good household management. A prudent wife or husband wouldn't think of grocery shopping without checking newspaper ads for coupons and specials. Any discount store will sell you a new camera or lens the same way. Just the other day I saw an ad for a brand new Minolta XE-7 with a 50mm fl.8 for $269.95; that's 30 dollars below dealer's net. The store was part of a chain and apparently had purchased a large number of units, thereby increasing the profit margin.

Sometimes you can make money by not taking an assignment! I can't count the number of times that photographer friends of mine have accepted a job simply because they're hired, even though the price bid is so low that the profit is negligible. The time would be better spent soliciting more profitable jobs. As I went up the financial ladder, I used to cut off the least profitable jobs from the bottom and add to the top, the newer, more lucrative assignments. But all of this should be elementary to you. *There is,* neverthe-less, one area where many of my photographer friends fall down.

This is the managing of credit or loan money. Let's say you are buying a new automobile to be used in your photographic business. You've found the car you want and have agreed on a trade-in price for your old car and the difference to be financed is $5,000. The dealer will usually charge a rate of 13.5 percent to as low as 11.25 percent. One of the reasons why he gave you such a good trade-in is that he gets a "kickback," or refund, from the bank, usually as much as 5 percent of the finance charge. This is figured in your deal when the dealer draws up the papers. Anyone who buys this way is bound to be trapped.

The best way to buy anything you need is to go to the bank and borrow the money to pay for the car. But even at the bank there are many alternatives. Borrowing on an "installment" loan does save you the dealer's cushion but again you could be still wast-ing money. The next best bank borrowing method is the "90-day note." The interest rate is lower, usually around 9–9½ percent, but you don't run into the "Rule of 78." What this rule means is that you're paying the highest rate of interest during the first month and the scale goes down each succeeding month. In effect, if you pay off within the first year, your "effective rate of interest" is actually higher than the rate you con-tracted for. You would have to go the full 24, 36 or 48 months of your installment loan contract to achieve the rate in the contract. The 90-day note, on the other hand, is a simple interest note, and you make either interest alone or interest and principal payments every 90 days. The responsibility to make payments is left up to you; you'd better be the type that can schedule and make payments without a payment book. Remember this: the bank can call that note or refuse to re-issue any time it wishes, though it rarely does.

The best way to borrow money is through the "passbook loan." The rate at the time of this writing is 2 to 3 percent above the rate of interest in your present savings account. Say you want $5,000 for a new car and you have a 5¼ percent savings account with $6,000 in it. You surrender your passbook for the term of your loan, but you don't lose the interest during that same term. Even though the contract will read 7¼ percent, your *net* cost is really 2 percent. That's exactly what you pay for borrowing $5,000. Again, you have to make your payments on a schedule of your own making. When you get your passbook back, you will see that your account has been credited with regular interest payments of 5¼ percent. Now, that's what I call managing your money.

So it pays to start or have some of your working capital in a savings bank, not a savings and loan or a commercial bank, but a savings bank. This money can be used as collateral for more than one loan and even two or three at the same time, all at 2 percent above your rate of interest. It would pay you to put your money in the certificate of deposit that pays the best interest. At this time that's 7¾ percent.

# 22 Intimidation

Client relations are as important to a photographic business as is bookkeeping, perhaps even more important. Yet little attention is devoted to understanding the psychological implications between photographers and their clients. There *is* a subterranean stream of activity below the surface of your day-to-day contacts that has an effect on your successes and failures.

Let's make some hypotheses. Suppose that your first contact with a prospect is a letter. Your prospect has one item by which to judge you as a person and as a professional photographer.

Your first contact must be designed and worded to create the impression you want your prospective client to have of you. You want him or her to feel that you're competent to do the assignment and can be depended upon to use creative imagination to go a step beyond the straight, focus-and-expose ordinary photographer.

First, the client examines the stationery; is it tastefully designed? printed or engraved? Does it suggest quality and prestige or does it smack of amateurishness and cheapness? Is the typewriter of *professional* quality, with crisp clear impressions, or are the characters fuzzy? Is the typing clean and accurate or error-filled and blotched with type-overs?

The language used also makes an impression. Are the sentences clear and well expressed? What about the grammar, the punctuation? Obviously, the spelling must be correct. If there are mistakes, are they corrected or left in? Are the corrections well made?

What you say is most important. There's a fine line between extravagant claims and a listing of prestigious credits or impressive photographic capabilities; you must choose one or the other, but not both. Either list your memberships, degrees and important awards related to your profession or use the area for advertising the types of photography you do.

When listing degrees, awards and memberships, be very careful not to sound pompous or overwhelming; use less than 10-point type and place the listings unobtrusively along the bottom of the sheet; it's best not to have them shout from the top of the page. If you haven't many credits, list your memberships in professional societies; this assures the client that you are a professional and not a dilettante. By awards, I don't mean a blue ribbon you may have won at your state convention but rather a national or international prize, grant, or honor that might be known by the recipient of your letter.

The next piece of material is the brochure, or flyer. Without advertising, it's almost impossible to make yourself known to clients unless you have a walk-in type portrait business, and even there, advertising makes the difference between success and just eking out an existence. If you are marketing color photographs, your brochure should be printed in color. A black and white brochure that advertises color photography simply doesn't ring true in the client's mind. Color is expensive, but if you use standard forms and you have an art director, not yourself, lay out the piece, a tasteful eight-picture brochure can be made inexpensively. Again, this piece must not be showy, but it must show your facilities; you must impress your client with the fact that you have the equipment to do the job, the facilities for processing and finishing and the capabilities to do the assignment well. This last thing can be shown by printed samples of successful work or the names of your other clients. Whatever you do, don't try to design your own stationery or flyers unless you are an artist. I always find it best to hire a professional, just as you would want my client to hire me, a professional.

Having set the stage with the letter and followed with the flyer or brochure, your next move is to get the client to visit your studio, if you have one, or to call on him or her. This call is most important. It's my opinion that anyone you intend to call on should already be acquainted with you through letters, brochures and telephone calls before this visit. This isn't to say a blind request for an appointment can't bring the desired results, but I'm convinced that the psychological impression created by a letter and a brochure has a great deal to do with acceptance by the client. This is especially true regarding price. For example, if I quote that a simple catalogue color transparency made in my studio is $250, and I quote this price on the telephone without the benefit of the client's being exposed to my studio or to my brochures, I *know* he's going to search elsewhere. However, if I can get him to the studio, or have softened him up with letters and brochures and established my credentials, the price will stick. Surprisingly, quality is not the only attraction by which people buy —preselling by psychological boosting often is. Of course, this assumes that there is a reasonable amount of quality available in the photograph.

Establishing your credentials is similarly important. This can greatly alter the relationship between the photographer and client. Before the client is aware of the credentials of the photographer, facilities and reputation, he was probably inclined to have a preconceived idea of the price and quality he wanted. After you establish yourself for him, the client is inclined to spend more.

Going to visit the client places you in a subordinate position as the seller. How you handle that important meeting determines your financial future— at least with that client. I remember an old Charlie Chaplin movie where the client had a chair with a raising rachet; if the visitor was taller than the client, the client raised his chair above his visitor's. In the movie, Chaplin had a rachet chair, too, so he and the client tried to out raise each other.

Today, the office is the "rachet." The client's plush carpet, large desk, huge judge's chair, as well as a formidable secretary or receptionist can insulate the client and place him or her in a superior position for intimidating the photographer. So the responsibility is yours to give an impression of competence and create an aura of dignity without pomposity. You must speak firmly, clearly, but without braggadocio to inspire your client's confidence. If you can survive intimidation from your client by handling yourself well, you'll probably get the job. The client is well aware of his effect of intimidation—it is calculated.

I practice intimidation myself. Clients who visit my office find that my studio walls simply boast of prestigious clients. Someone coming in with the idea of spending $250 can easily be elevated to $500. Of course, it sometimes has the opposite effect; a client may feel that he or she can't afford me. By graciously pointing out the value of not having to do a job over, by combining uses of photography, and by showing the client that I am an expert on designing the photographic assignment to fit his needs, I can sometimes convince him otherwise. Quite often a photographer is capable of the photographic part of the assignment, but unable to advise the client on the best way to go in reproduction.

All of this leads back to my bête noire—telephone quoting. I simply won't do it, except on rare occasion. It offers no psychological advantage. I dislike to call on the client also, but that's because I have a large, well-designed studio. When I was just building my studio and my reputation, I had to make calls—but my calls were productions. Where other photographers showed a carousel of slides, I asked for the conference room and staged a production of thirty 20 × 24 dye transfer prints complete with lights for proper viewing. In a sense, I avoided the client's office, turned his conference room into a gallery, and altered our relationship to where I was psychologically superior—at least for the moment.

You might call this "psyching the client."

# 23 Speculative Photo-Graphic Illustration

Photographers anticipating going into the photographic business should investigate the philosophy of speculation. This is especially appropriate for newer members of the profession and small studios beset with rising costs, increased competition and the proliferation of professionals. Perhaps a small definition of what I mean by "speculation" is in order: what I mean is not portraiture or even commercial photography but that area I call "illustration"; that is, photographs for greeting cards, posters, record albums, book jackets and the thousands upon thousands of background photographs used in the "blister-packaging" of products seen in every discount store in the world. There are numerous advantages to such a way of photographic livelihood:

1. You need not be located in a specific section of the country such as a metropolitan area or a downtown location with high-density traffic, since your client contacts are by mail.

2. You need no studio with specialized equipment to go with it nor any studio "appointments" with backgrounds and furnishings; no expensive-to-heat high-ceilinged area for commercial photography and no props. You may need a small area for your own shooting as well as an apartment or house basement darkroom and, of course, an office.

3. The world is your market and your clients are everywhere and easily reached by mail. You are not dependent on existing industries where you presently live nor does your income rise and fall randomly or with their fortunes. A depressed economic situation in your area will have little effect on your business.

4. You will own your own photographs, as you will sell only reproduction rights. A wide variety of clients will buy reproduction rights. However, this places a heavy responsibility on you to perfect your duping technique.

5. Relatively little equipment is necessary. It's entirely possible to operate such a business successfully with one 35mm camera and a few lenses. Much too much money is wasted on "gadgetry"—rationalized and justified by the photographer's ego. If equipment were considered tools rather than toys, you'd be surprised at how little is really needed.

6. If the photographs are carefully thought out and are timeless, they can be sold over and over again through repeated mailings to innumerable clients all

over the world. A good transparency can sell for 20 or even more years, becoming an "annuity" to the photographer.

7. Speculation such as I suggest requires no high-salaried employees, uses little energy, isn't affected by competition, is generally inexpensive to perform and is easily the most efficient way to function as a photographer.

However, if you can't discipline yourself, or if you are compulsively lazy and need to be constantly prodded, then this is not for you. You perhaps need a boss, a demanding client or someone else to tell you what to do. In *this* system you take the photographs you like and want to make, and you rarely follow the dictates of others, even when such speculation begets assignments.

Assignments are generated by such mailings. Because you have shown that you're able to perform exceptionally well, art directors and editors give you a minimal amount of direction. This again is highly prized and most desirable, but, as we've seen in earlier chapters, you must learn how to stimulate your imagination.

# 24 Spatial Impressions As First Aid

In my lectures years ago, I used to say that if you can't make your photographs good, then make them big; and if they still aren't too good, frame 'em. This used to bring much laughter and applause. Although I said that calculating to stimulate my audience, I sometimes think the point was missed in the jocularity.

Surprisingly, there are many ways of improving the overall impression of your photographs besides the common methods of matting, framing and making them big. Placing just two together improves both. Making a wall of photographs again improves each one. As you add more photographs to your display, the overall effect is usually enhanced. Such

155

points have to be considered even if you are just showing a portfolio. The portfolio then becomes the showcase or the reception room of your studio.

Let's go back for a moment and discuss some relevant side issues. For instance, have you noticed that 99 percent of all models' composites are in black and white? Have you ever wondered why? The reason is that art directors and photographers who buy modeling time want whatever qualities the model has to show in the simplest form of photography—black and white. No adornments or frills, and no attempt to dress up the photograph. What he or she has must show without the benefit of color, size, matting or framing. Using black and white photos for this purpose is so accepted that to attempt anything else is to risk being labeled incompetent. Models' composites are so standardized by the big agencies that the quality of the model's ability and the photographer's expertise is apparent. If a model is even the slightest bit inept at posing, it will be evident in simple black and white photographs.

Conversely, this implies that the use of color, matting, and so on, can disguise technical flaws in the posing or in the physical attributes of the model. I say it can.

Let's carry this hypothesis a step further. Some of the world's most acclaimed photography is in black and white—for the very reasons outlined above. No subterfuge of color, matting and so on can be used to disguise inadequate photographic technique. This isn't to say that all color photography is disguising something; quite the contrary. When an expert judges color he or she can see the effects of a technician and his discipline, but that requires the ability to make expert diagnoses, something often far beyond the average critic.

Quite often a lecturer on the photographic circuit will use such techniques to his own advantage. He appears with a huge display of photographs, usually framed. There's nothing wrong or pretentious about this; he's just making the best presentation he can. But you, the viewer, may be *subliminally* impressed in "seeing" more quality than is really there.

I use a plethora of large color photographs in my own lectures to bring out specific points relating to the way in which I practice photography. That's the overt use, but I'm also well aware of the subliminal impression of magnificence I create—frankly, it's contrived. Again, I bring this point out in the lecture so that there is no chance of the lesson's being lost. In fact, that lesson is the point of the lecture.

When an art director designs an ad, he selects the size of the type as well as its shape or style and, further, he designs the type to fit a certain space. He uses a headline in one size and style and a subhead in another and the body copy may very well be in a third. The type should complement the illustration— photographic or hand art—and then the two, type and illustration, are arranged together on the page to create a harmonious entity.

Sometimes the art director selects the page on which the ad is to appear, verso or recto (left or right). There might be border art, framing or matting of some sort; each component is carefully coordinated with the others so as to create a specific desired impression. The overall impression is designed to motivate the consumer to buy the product or service.

Interior decorators always make sure that each individual item—piece of furniture, floor covering, wallpaper, paint, drapes and accessories—works with each other item and that all together, they work as a group. Quite often, the uninitiated decorator will create a hodge-podge of miscellanea by mixing periods, styles and origins; this shows as discordance, fairly bellowing at the knowledgeable observer, offending his sense of aesthetic harmony.

Interestingly, under such a cacophony, the individual pieces lose whatever quality they have to the overall effect. The photographer must be just as aware as a brilliant decorator of the relationship of one print on the wall to another, and another and so on; he must also consider things such as drapes, furniture, floor covering and even the architectural style of the space. Even the size of each photograph is critical to the overall effect, but it is the largest photographs that seem to draw the most attention and, further, seem to be considered as the best by critics—and that means customers, also.

Pick up the latest issue of your favorite photographic magazine and turn to a spread or portfolio of prints. Study the two-page layout carefully, and then tear out the pages and scissor the pictures out of context and study each one individually. Quite astonishingly, you'll notice that the single photograph isn't as great as you thought it was when it was part of the two-page layout. Actually, you may suspect that the single photograph was dull. Now you should notice the talented hand of an art director in the two-page spread. This is another reason why you should hire a professional art director to design your sales pieces, brochures or posters.

You may very well have to work backwards when designing a studio. I'm talking about style. Style is that elusive, almost indescribable quality that differentiates us one from another. Every photographer, no matter how inchoate, develops an individual style early and, generally, but not always, his or her taste reflects that style. If the two are homogeneous, then he or she becomes successful. Disharmony of style creates a clashing of sensibilities within the viewer that offends the senses, including one's sense of taste and—perhaps even one's sense of smell.

If you don't have or don't develop style along with a sense of harmony and balance in your photography, you won't become successful. But these things can be learned; in the meantime, if you can't make 'em good, make 'em big; if they still need help, mat 'em; if they need more help, frame 'em.

# 25 The Planned Disaster

Recently, when I was visiting a professional photographer's studio, I heard him discussing a job with a client, who was apparently asking for photographs of workers in a foundry. This in itself is not extraordinary, but the client was asking for black and white prints, color prints and color transparencies. Whenever I hear such requests I become wary. I can smell a "planned disaster."

I heard this photographer toadying to the client, agreeing almost without question. He was well on the way to a planned disaster. He had decided on the phone that he'd use extra film magazines, one for each kind of film he'd use: "Yes, Sir, I'll be able to get the photographs you want, etc., etc." Well, the truth is he wouldn't.

Almost all businessmen professional photographers try to be agreeable. After all, there are financial obligations to running a studio or even a freelance operation. But this business of "being agreeable" to whatever the client says without question leads to enormous problems and usually a failure to satisfy the client.

The photographer either just wasn't thinking or he didn't know better. Various kinds of photographs he will take "simultaneously", won't be the same, unless he is posing inanimate objects, but certainly not factory workers. Factory workers labor at a "piece rate"; they don't stop for anybody. Changing backs on a camera, most likely a Hassie, slows the photographer down to where he doesn't have the time to do much creative photography; his mind is so busy with the mechanical calculations of coordinating exposure, lighting, and the physical manipulation of his camera that he has little time to concentrate on the subject.

I knew and I think he knew that his best bet was to use the new Vericolor Professional Type "S," which easily makes the best color prints; he could make excellent black and white prints with the Panalure paper; with the new Vericolor Print Film (4111) he would have some surprisingly high quality transparencies. His reluctance to "go this way" stemmed from his lack of ability to print each of these types. He could make the color prints easily enough; perhaps even the black and white prints—they're not that tricky, but he was stumped when it came to the transparencies. Too bad. These films are of the newer generation and have some characteristics that make them even more desirable than original photography exposed directly in the camera.

Even if he didn't want to get involved with the processing, there's nothing difficult in employing any of these films and using a modern professional laboratory; and there are some decidedly advantageous reasons for using color negatives in the first place.

To be able to respond to the needs of clients, a professional photographer must be able to use all types of materials. He must not use them as crutches to pull him out of an awkward situation; he must use them to expand the scope of his capabilities.

For instance, there are occasions where using a color negative to get to a color transparency is the best method. One example of this method is a case in which the interior, such as a foundry, has little or no color. A straight shot on transparency material would yield a flat rather dull chrome. A color negative can be printed or manipulated to enhance existing color. Where little lighting is available, a color negative can be overexposed and "dodged" to even out the lighting on the print film, thereby yielding a higher quality chrome than you would using transparency material originally.

Much of the professionals' reluctance to do the printing stems from the fact that most of them believe that you must have an analyzer to print print film. This is not generally so. Print film differs from negative film in that one balance usually handles all properly exposed and processed negative films. Please take this with a grain of salt because although there's one balance it will have slight variations depending on how good the negative is. But the problem is not nearly so critical as making a print from a color negative—and even that is getting easier every day. In the old days (up till last year) processing these color materials required different chemical formulas; C-22, C-41 or, in the case of internegative film, a modification of the first developer. These variations frightened the timorous . . . and not a few professionals.

All of this has changed. For instance, color negative film, color internegative film, and color print film can all be developed in C-41, simultaneously and for the same developing time. And also, the number of steps has decreased and the total working time has been shortened.

My friend's problem would have been complicated somewhat by the client's asking for 35mm slides, as he probably would have just a few short years back. Today's emulsions are far superior to those of even a year ago; they are finer grained, have better color response and are less affected by temperature. So now, using 35mm wouldn't present much of a problem.

Can you imagine our poor professional working alone trying to handle lighting, various backs on the camera, and possibly a second camera if the client wanted 35mm slides. And he'd have the client beating in his ear and the workers shouting: "Hey! take my picture." With such complications, it is no wonder some photographers become studio catalogue specialists, where everything is under one roof.

The client should be questioned to determine exactly what is to be the end use of the photographs. Sometimes, especially if he is an art director, the client asks for a special film or may even request that you use a specific lens. Here, he may be trying to appear knowledgeable. More often you'll find that he requests a certain size camera system. These options rightfully belong to the photographer. To keep the client happy you must carefully determine exactly what is in his mind and, if there is a misconception, diplomatically make the right suggestions *before* going out on the assignment, lest you wind up with a planned disaster.

# 26 Learn to Say No

Until you learn to say no to customers, you're never going to succeed in the business of photography. I just finished talking on the phone with a commercial studio owner who employs one full-time and one half-time person, pays rent of $500 a month for his studio and pays about the same for his home. He's in the never, never land of in-between. I'd call it a trap. He'll never make any money until he makes some changes.

In this business of photography, you either have to make your business grow to the point where you have enough employees so that they generate a gross income that will support you, or you must be so small that you have little or no overhead and you yourself generate the work and ultimately the income. The in-between is full of futile traps, and unwary photographers fall into them regularly.

Our errors are the product of our beginnings in photography. When we began, we tried desperately to sell, sell, sell; every job we could get was needed. Some jobs were tiny, but it didn't matter—sell, after all, if you're going to crank up the developer or the enlarger you might just as well do another job since you can run them together. Sheer nonsense. Each job has to be highly profitable, unrelated to whether or not you can save money by running those films with something else.

Some jobs should never be accepted under any circumstances. In this category are those that have a small gross. Reprinting is an occupational disease that drives me up the wall. I gave up the negatives years ago. I want only original photography; I simply won't crank up a darkroom for $10 or $20, or not even for anything under $100.

If any employer asked you to stay for a few extra hours, gratis, you'd be indignant. But you'll think nothing of staying over to finish a job for a favorite customer, and I don't think you'll add any double time to the bill, either.

It's understood in this day and age that the work week is about forty hours; when was the last time you worked exactly forty hours for yourself (not a salaried job)? You have such a love for the work of photography that you're willing to work night and day. If you figured out your rate of pay, it'd look more like $1 an hour. So, you just shut your eyes to those figures and rationalize about "responsibility to the customer" or "If I do this now, I won't have to come in tomorrow." Nonsense. You'll be there tomorrow just the same, because something else always has to be done.

Photography is a "profession" that seems to have more things to do every time you turn around. If you respond to everyone who comes to you for work, you'll work yourself into the grave. And love every minute of it.

I've written such criticisms of the business of photography for years, and photographers often call me up to say I'm right, but then they go right back to doing things the old way. *Must* take care of their customers. *Must* "service" the account. There's a recession on, you know. Mustn't offend the customers, they'll go somewhere else.

The hard points of a photographic life are these:

Cut off the lower paying jobs at the bottom of your list as you add on new and more expensive work at the top. Look over every phase of your photographic business and do so with the jaundiced eye of an efficiency expert. Better still, call in a professional photographer friend and level with him. Show him your books and analyze each job you're doing. Examine your work flow for waste and errors. How much mail can you handle? Are you the Post Office?

Is your buying planned or haphazard? Do you buy in quantity and deep freeze your film and paper, or do you buy impulsively? Are you a collector of pretty gadgets called cameras and accessories? Why do you have so many cameras when you need only two or three? Why is it you have a scillion filters when you could have planned your purchases properly and had one or two sets that would fit all your lenses? Are there any cameras lying about that aren't used anymore? Why don't you sell them? Do you have any equipment at all that is obsolete and is just stored on the off-chance that you might need it someday? Have you ever had to throw out film or paper because you changed your mind about using it or it went out of date? Are you a collector of expensive photographic junk? Do you have old stationery? Would you be loathe to show such an efficiency bug as I around your studio knowing my bald-eagle-eye would pick out flaws everywhere I looked?

If you answered yes to any of the above, you know you have trouble. So what do you do? Besides the obvious, and I won't bore you with answers to the above since they should be self-evident, you have to develop new ways of thinking. In general this is what to think about:

At the beginning of this diatribe, I mentioned the importance of not getting trapped with a studio too small for the employees to make a profit for you. The theory here is that you need somewhere around five or more productive employees before they can generate enough money to make a profit for you. With one or two, in general, you run around finding work for them, which wastes your time and bothers the hell out of them. Effectively, you are working for your employees for two main reasons. The first is the time you spend away from what you're doing taking care of finding work for them or filling out state or federal forms related to having employees—those forms take one day out of every week. The other reason is that you must generate enough work to warrant employing people in the first place.

If you have high overhead, such as rent, light, heat and a myriad of other things, figure another day or so of work to pay for them. If there's anything left for you to live on, it's a miracle. Little wonder that so many of the photographers in the United States live from hand to mouth.

The way around all this is, as I mentioned before, the bigger studio or, as I chose, the smaller. Work for yourself and do all the work yourself. Combine your photographic studio or place of business with your home. This cuts your expenses enormously and gives you a deduction on taxes. Be very selective with the work you do and send out all the work that is just drudgery to you to the labs; accept no job unless it is profitable, and highly profitable. Treat your cameras and other photographic apparatus as tools, not icons to be worshipped; bend them to your will and stop buying everything invented. If you find you are a compulsive photophile and must own every new invention, then sell an old one almost as soon as you buy a new one. Fortunately, inflation is working for you (sheer heresy)! The equipment you bought three years ago is worth about the same as what you paid for it—if you sell it immediately.

Pick your own customers and go after them, not just anyone who happens along. Learn to be an assignment photographer and get paid for your expenses. Raise your rates! Keep raising them until you lose customers. Remember, chop off from the bottom and keep after the more prestigious and more affluent clients. Drop those who don't pay within thirty days, as you can't afford to finance them.

Finally, until you learn to say no, your yesses will just nail you more tightly into the trap.

# 27 Time: The Critical Resource

We all talk about the evils of wasted energy, but nothing is so precious as time. Water and gasoline may be easier to understand as energy sources and their waste is continuing at an alarming rate, so that most assuredly we shall all have to pay the piper for our wanton misuse of these vital elements of our way of life. But nothing, nothing can possibly compare with our enormous wastage of *time.* Yet *waste of time* is really a misnomer, as one can't really waste time. Time marches on inexorably, the clock ticking away each second, each minute and each hour relentlessly. No, we can't waste *time,* we waste the *management* and the opportunities of time. We can manage time only by managing ourselves. If we could learn to manage properly our use of time, we would be saving more energy than we would by saving all the gasoline and water that we waste.

Photographers are rarely trained in business practice—a well-known fact—but they are masters of business administration when one compares this knowledge to their knowledge and mastery of managing time. It matters not whether they're a one-person business, a moonlighter in photography or the president of a studio employing one or more persons—they must learn to manage not only their time but that of their employees. Yet if you asked one how much time he spends working, you'd find, more often than not, that he will give you a figure far above the standard 40 hours a week. He'll say this with pride, a martyr to his cause, and be injured by your saying that he might work a normal week. But if you examine his—or perhaps your own—week, listing each task and the amount of time spent on it, you'll find that precious little is accomplished in relation to the time available. As Seneca said, "He is most powerful who has power over himself." It is this power over ourselves that we must develop—the power to control our use of time.

Perhaps one of the best ways is to learn to manage yourself by removing internally generated time wasters, and this requires changing habits. If you examine your habits carefully, you will find that many of them are nothing more than time wasters. We need to make automatic or habitual as many useful actions as we can. The more daily routines we can make a matter of habit the more time we will have for creative or imaginative planning.

One enemy of good habits is *indecision.* To deliberate over each minute task or refuse to delegate responsibility is to misuse managerial power. A manager who displays indecision will never have the time to invent, will never create, and will never contribute to his own well-being or that of his employees.

*Procrastination*—the avoidance of an unpleasant or unwanted task—is a close relative of incompetence and the handmaiden of inefficiency. Photographers who procrastinate welcome interruptions; such diversions serve to put off the task at hand. Many photographers go out for coffee with every sales person who calls, much to their own detriment. Making a timely decision and disposing of a task is the mark of a successful manager. Time is often mismanaged by employees; for instance, by extending the task to fit the time instead of fitting the time to the task.

Here are some guidelines for better time management:

1. Learn to organize your tasks each morning.
2. Give each task a priority.
3. Try to concentrate on one task at a time and finish it.
4. Give yourself a deadline for each task.
5. Don't duck a difficult problem; force yourself to approach it.
6. Analyze your working habits and get rid of the bad ones.
7. Don't be a perfectionist. You will frustrate yourself and your employees.

Admittedly, these things are easier said than done, but such a guide is used by major corporations for their executives. It applies to anyone.

*Concentration* on tasks is difficult if your office procedure allows interruptions. If you develop the habit of opening the mail first (a good habit since the mail might contain orders that will affect the day's business), then see that telephone calls are held and grouped for your convenience. After all, concentrated effort over a protracted period can be more productive than a momentary flash of genius. A sense of accomplishment will be one result of your discipline. "Know thyself," as Socrates said. If you feel you can't concentrate, can't create good habits or can't get rid of bad ones, then you may need psychological help or at least solid advice.

In a small business, employees mimic or become reflections of the manager; if the manager is slack or a procrastinator, if he is disorganized or has poor working habits, he will infect his employees. If he can organize his working habits and discipline himself, he will be able to spread these habits by example to his workers.

I suggest you devise two checklists of time wasters. The first containing externally imposed wasters:

1. The telephone.
2. A lack of setting priorities for daily tasks.
3. Employees with problems.
4. Inefficient office procedures or word-processing.
5. Constant interruptions—being too available to people who drop by.
6. Interminable and unnecessary meetings.
7. Poor communications.
8. Mistakes caused by haste and inefficiency.

9. Management by crisis—when procrastination allows avoidable problems to develop.
10. Taking on routine tasks that could be accomplished by others.
11. Acting prematurely on incomplete information.

The second list might contain self-generating items such as:

1. Attempting too many tasks at once.
2. A general lack of organization of your desk.
3. Being unable to say no.
4. Delegating responsibility without delegating authority.
5. Placing inefficient managers in positions of authority.
6. Bypassing your own chain-of-command, which causes confusion.
7. Making hasty decisions—the consequence of action without thought is usually chaos.
8. And, of course, procrastination.

Assuming you and the members of your organization are not time wasters, or that you accomplish the task of organizing yourself and your time, what do you do with the time gained?

I can answer this question from my own experience.

Years ago I operated as a commercial studio with about five employees. The studio was successful from the financial point of view but I felt I had lost touch with creative photography, the mystique and fascination that had caused me to choose photography over a career in medicine. I had become a business manager, tied to my desk, performing business tasks, finding work for my employees, spending hours on the telephone either soliciting business or solving client-photographer problems. At the end of the day, I was too exhausted for photography as a hobby as well as for my family life. About fifteen years ago, I broke that pattern. It took time, but bit by bit, I switched my photographic business to making photographs that I liked. I no longer was "open for business" locally. It has now been five years since I've had a single employee. And the result?

I can take time to *think*. I can and do study before an assignment. I research each task. I spend a great deal of time performing creative tasks that are enormously rewarding. I work at my own pace—this has meant breaking the habits of years. Sometimes I work early in the morning and read for the entire afternoon. I've discovered that reading and studying are part of my working life and I jealously guard that time. I put the answering machine on most of the time and telephone only when I have several calls to make. I "play" in the darkroom uninterrupted by calls or customers. Salespeople have long since given up calling. My income? It's down, but then I don't have the salaries of employees and the expenses a staff generates in the form of additional taxes. I am far more creative, far more organized, far more capable as a photographer, and far happier than I've ever been. I don't recommend my regimen for all, because it requires constant attention to self-discipline and although I've been doing this for many years I find I can backslide, but the longer I work on developing good working habits, the easier my work becomes.

Sow a thought, and you reap an act.
Sow an act, and you reap a habit.
Sow a habit, and you reap a character.
Sow a character, and you reap a destiny.

—Anonymous

# 28 The Photographic Control Commission

"**H**ello. I'm from the *Photographic Control Commission License Bureau.* May I speak with you for a few minutes?"

"Uh, of course, come in. My license is in order, I renewed, I think I did, uh, Mary, didn't we renew our license a couple of months ago? Seems to me I remember sending in the check."

"Excuse me, Mr. Perry, it's not your license I want to talk to you about. Your basic license is in order. The problem is in your subspecialty, Commercial Photography. We have a complaint that you alledgedly sold some photographs that were used for greeting cards. You know that is illegal."

177

"Well, all I did was take some mood photographs and . . ."

"The law is pretty specific about that, Mr. Perry. You're licensed to practice Commerical Photography only—in black and white and color. I have the list here and it includes such subjects as catalogues of products, construction progress, brochures and postcards, photographs of machinery, but not industrial as that . . ."

"But how did you . . ."

"From a photographer in the Illustration subspecialty. He called on a client who was a greeting card manufacturer. The client praised some slides he purchased, he said, from you. The client is not responsible; he can purchase where he wishes. So this illustrator turned your name in and I'm . . ."

"The dirty rat! If I catch him I'll . . ."

"Now, now, come now, Mr. Perry, you know that won't do you any good. The PCC would frown on your taking a vindictive attitude. After all, we depend on the vast majority of licensed photographers to let us know when someone steps out of line. We can't police the entire photographic establishment. Back when licensing first came in in 1981, you photographers wanted to be protected from 'unfair business practices,' and so far it has worked well."

"But I think it's restrictive. Besides, it stifles creativity."

"You should have thought of that back in 1981. Another thing, Mr. Perry. We've had complaints that you took photographs in another state without that state's permit."

"I was on vacation, and I saw a really gorgeous sunset, and I . . ."

"You know that scenics are not in your specialty, Mr. Perry. You had no right to take that photograph, even if . . ."

"But I didn't intend to sell it. I wanted it as a decoration for my own . . ."

"That doesn't matter. You know you have to get a permit from the PCC of the state and file a copy of the photograph with them and an affidavit sworn to and notarized that you intend to use the photograph yourself and that you don't intend to sell it. Our informant saw you by the side of the road with a tripod and camera, a sure sign of a violation . . ."

"But I didn't *sell* it . . ."

"Still, you violated Chapter IX, Section 32 paragraph (a) 1: 'No photographer shall knowingly take or make a photograph in another state other than the state in which he or she is licensed without obtaining a permit and filing a notarized affidavit swearing that he or she will not attempt to sell or give away a copy, a print, a slide or any other type of reproduction and further that a copy of each and every exposure shall be filed with the state within 30 days of the original exposure. Violators of this section are subject to disciplinary action by the grievance committee of the Photographic Control Commission of the aggrieved state, and punitive measures shall include a suspension of photographic privileges for a period of 30 days and a fine of $100. For a first offense. Second or third offenders are subject to indefinite suspension.' This is a section of the *National Unfair Photographic Practices Act of 1981, U.S. Title Code.*"

"If I fill out an affidavit now and give you a copy of the photograph, would that satisfy you?"

"I'm afraid I couldn't do that Mr. Perry. You see,

you not only violated the *State Act of the Photographic Control Commission,* but you violated the *National Unfair Photographic Practices Act.* I'm just a state inspector and I don't have the right to abrogate the law of the Federal Government."

"Listen, if I turn state's evidence, would you . . . maybe forget this? If I gave you the names of some photographers that I know are violating both state and Federal Acts . . . I could give you information about where they sold the photographs and . . . get this! . . . I could give you documentation of the prices —and the prices were under those of the *Schedule of Allowable Prices, National Unfair Photographic Practices Act!"*

"Well, I'm not allowed to make deals with offenders, but I could put in a good word . . . I could say you cooperated with the Commission and that would count . . . but what kind of violations are you talking about?"

"Well, I know of a licensed Baby Photographer who solicited parents outside of his established area. And, I know of Catholic Photographers who photograph Jewish weddings. . . ."

"Go on. Those are good, but I'd need more."

"Then how about an Annual Report Photographer who took a photograph for a client that was used for an advertisement?"

"Good, very good."

"And . . . I know a Passport Specialist who sold a portrait without a permit—and you know that is taboo."

"Well, Mr. Perry, I can see that maybe you're the type of upstanding photographer the PCC admires. You certainly have the right attitude, and I'll see that you are given credit for this information, but first it must be documented—you know—the names, dates, places and the people involved. This would put a feather in my cap, all right, to come up with half a dozen violators instead of one small violator like you. You might just be eligible for the IR, you know, the Informant's Reward, for turning in your fellow photographers. Let's get down to the documentation, okay, Mr. Perry?"

*     *     *

*This may very well sound like a spoof to you, yet what you have just read is possibly just around the corner, if you don't do anything about it. Many photographers, bothered by what they term as "unfair competition," have asked their state associations for some form of licensing, and, in fact, one state does have a modest licensing law. My satire is in the extreme in order to show you what can happen when overzealous people filled with righteous indignation persuade their law makers to pass restrictive measures governing the practice of photography. The trouble with laws is that the original intent is distorted in the writing and then abuses abound.*

# 29 The Modernization of the Photographer

It's amazing how we as a nation have become machine oriented. Convenience gadgetry, most of which used to be considered luxury items just a few short years ago, are now necessities. We're all aware of the improvements in home appliances, and even the lowly office has become glamorized. For example you don't "type" letters, memos, drafts, purchase orders and invoices—you "word process" them. And every other moment you find you need a duplicate of something or other; copies here, copies there, copies everywhere. We certainly live in the age of the paper blizzard.

I started using the IBM Executive typewriter in the early 1950s, shortly after it appeared on the market, because I was using the carbon ribbon feature to print my own brochures or at least make "camera-ready" copy for printing. In those days, an expenditure of $350 for a typewriter was a major equipment investment, particularly for a photographer. I remember writing an article for Charlie Abel's early photographic magazine, *The Professional Photographer* (the precursor of the present-day magazine of the same name), on the advantages of modern office equipment. In those days I had a copier that cost about $100 and had anyone suggested that I might spend much more than that on a copier I would said that was nonsense. I now have a $4,000 copier that prints on my stationery, both sides of any kind of paper, makes mailing labels, overhead projector transparencies, and even some rather sophisticated black and white high-contrast prints from my screened half-toned photographic prints. I also have a $6,000 word-processing station. The strangest thing is that I can't figure out how I got along without such tools all these years.

The point is that if we wish to make a profitable operation out of our photographic business we must modernize our offices just as we modernize our photographic equipment. Even a two-man photographer's office needs these tools—particularly because these are labor-saving devices and labor is an expensive commodity. Few photographers are even aware that their offices are outdated. They may be the first in town to own the new Stranaflex-XF-17, but they are completely in the dark about new office equipment. Photographers rationalize that having a new lens or camera is something that will make better photographs, and hence more money. This is perhaps a vanity they really can't afford. But they're suspicious of any labor-saving device for the office. The office is a poor relation.

Just the other day I caught myself imagining that I had a need for one of the new microcomputers. Just as LED, quartz watches, and pocket calculators have become so popular in the last five years, so the new home computers will be in every office within the next five years. Computer stores are being franchised all across the country; they'll soon be as ubiquitous as McDonald's Golden Arches. These new computers are not toys—even though some can be programmed to play numerous games through your television set or on their own display screens. But make no mistake; they are another vital tool in the performance of office functions. I can't think of any more important acquisition than a microcomputer for a photographer to own.

The problem in selling these devices to the public is that people generally know so little about what these computers will do and how they are useful. The "toy" capability is better known and tends to denegrate the usefulness in the minds of the public. The direct application in solving photographic problems is not completely known.

It can't be long before the first ad will appear in *The Professional Photographer* for a computer programmer who will offer, for a fee, to program your microcomputer to solve many office as well as photographic problems.

The "chip," or "microprocessor," is the core of a host of new inventions, many of which will apply to the photographic profession. Meters, timers, programmers, temperature and pH probes and many more, are just a few of the newer instruments using the "chip." This chip is spawning a whole family of new electronic gadgets for home and business. The silicon chip is no bigger than your fingernail, yet it contains hundreds of thousands of "bits" of information and it will continue to revolutionize the way of life in the home and office. It'll be interesting to see what other space-age invention is around the corner and how it can aid us.

With the high cost of film, especially in the larger sheet film sizes, there is a need for a studio microcomputer. All the variables of exposure will be fed into the computer, which will process the data and give us all sorts of precise information about exposure, readout on a screen and, for the record, a hard-copy readout as well. Such items as bellows draw, reciprocity failure of the film, filter factors, lighting and lighting ratios, depth of field and even the color temperature will all be fed into the computer. The resultant readout will be the corrections in filtration for reciprocity and color temperature, exposure increase for bellows, and even a factor for shutter-speed error. Who knows? Perhaps we'll hook the microcomputer to the camera and let it read the exposure on the film as the exposure takes place, just as the Olympus OM-2 camera does now.

That's an interesting thought. Olympus OM-2 has a camera metering system that accurately reads the exposure on film and from the film as the exposure takes place, so why can't we have that *existing* technology, only in a separate meter-probe to do the same thing on larger format cameras? We need this microcomputer to narrow down the waste of color film.

Carry that same hypothesis into the darkroom where enormous amounts of color paper are wasted in trial exposures and color balances. It is ludicrous that we should continue to tolerate such waste, especially when the technology already exists at the large photo-finishing labs. It simply hasn't filtered down to the smaller user yet. Cibachrome paper costs about two dollars for an 11 × 14 sheet. Wasting two or three sheets is unacceptable regardless of the old sop that the client will pay for it. I'm a consumer, too, and I'm tired of having costs passed on to me. Photographer-customer relations aside, even when making prints for our own use we should not have to make more than one at the enlarger.

Let's think about color processing of films. The halcyon days of E-3 are gone. No longer can you develop in ambient room temperature or approximately 75°F. The new processing temperatures are as high as 105°F. At 75°F you could take your liquid chemicals off the shelf, mix them with water and expect the temperature not to fluctuate more than a degree or two in either direction, depending on whether you had a cool or warm darkroom. Since the stock chemicals and the water were at approximately the same temperature, your mixed solution was close to the using temperature. This is not so with the new 100-degree chemistry. The stock solutions are at 75°F and the water has to be over 120°F to compensate. Each solution that you mix has a different temperature since the ratio varies between the temperature and volume of the stock solution. This means a different temperature for each mixed solution. A computer in the darkroom could very easily tell you how much of what degree water will mix with how much liquid at 75°F to give you 105°F of mixed solution. This is just one example of one major chore in the darkroom.

The problem with most of the new electronic equipment is that it's obsolete almost from the day you buy it, probably because the manufacturers are hurried by the competition to get into the market as soon as possible. No one likes to enter a saturated market. Most new items shouldn't be purchased on the first go-around; they're almost always "improved" six months later. Even knowing this, I almost always jump on the new equipment bandwagon. I've known this, and I'm ever wary, but then I love photography and some of the gadgetry is awfully fascinating. Remember, too, there's no time when products are not being improved upon. Some notable exceptions are the Hassleblad camera systems, Olympus, Omega, and Linhof to name just a few whose manufacturers have a sense of responsibility and tend to make all their new items modular and compatible with existing equipment. This is a laudable procedure by very responsible manufacturers. Retooling for new products entails horrendous expense—but technology will be served. I'm still waiting for the new Hassleblad Laser camera, the Olympus Tri-Dimensional camera, the new Minolta camera that will process 35mm color transparency film in the camera similar to Panavision by Polaroid, and Polaroid Print Easels for enlargers and a host of other products.

But the next important piece of equipment still is definitely the mini- or microcomputer.

# 30 The Coloroid Dry Process Corporation

**N**ever heard of it? Of course you haven't, but it's just about here. The products they will make are vital to you as a professional photographer, and as a businessman-photographer you'd better heed this warning. The Coloroid Corporation makes dry process color materials for photographers; they started out making materials for the amateur snapshot market and had the market pretty much to themselves for almost 30 years when another photographic giant joined the market with similar products. This fact in itself is neither earth-shaking nor even important to you, but the professional items are. For instance, look at these products and the effect each will have on your operation. Remember that all of these products exist today in the research department of at least two corporations.

Instant snapshots exist in the form of Polacolor II and Kodak Instant color prints. These products are on the market. Already available is an 8 × 10 instant color print, dry processed. This means that for those of us who are in catalogue, industrial or illustrative photography, a creative photograph can be made with an 8 × 10 camera and the print processed instantly. These prints are grainless and correctable with cc filters. The impact of this one process is such as to threaten our present practices. Art directors may have a print suitable for engraving shortly after the photograph is taken. Models can be held while the print is being made and, once checked and found satisfactory, released. Do-overs, the bane of the commercial photographer, are almost extinct. Even if the process were used for layout purposes only, it would still be worth the time and expense. At present the process depends on a machine-driven processing unit with a total processing time of not more than two minutes. The colors are well saturated and the contrast is more than acceptable. Among its other uses would be any assignment away from a studio where expensive models and props would make it almost mandatory that the photographer check his exposure, and to have the final print would be a real blessing.

Also available soon are the 4 × 5 and 8 × 10 color transparencies processed either in the camera or in a dry motor-driven processor portable enough to be used in the studio while the shooting is taking place. Again, this means that color film processing as we know it is going to change, and for the better. No expensive processors with all sorts of chemicals to mix, not to speak of the savings in material, time and overhead.

The professional photographers are the stepchildren of photography, since the real money for manufacturers is in the amateur market. The Coloroid Corporation is not beholding to the photo-finishing industry as are other manufacturers. This indicates that they can move into the void and service professional photography with a line of professional products such as the two mentioned above and two more, without conflict with the photo-finisher.

Large color prints require expensive enlargers and processing equipment as well as facilities for the mixing and handling of the chemicals involved. The Coloroid Corporation has a dry process photographic color print system that would enable a photographer to make any enlargements up to and including 20 × 24 without the need for wet sinks or chemicals. The print would be exposed as it is now, in an enlarger, but the print would be in its processor—a motor-driven easel that would process the print instantly and with the color saturation, contrast and grainlessness of the present Polacolor II.

There's no question that 4 × 5 and 8 × 10 color transparencies processed in or near the camera would be of enormous value to the professional photographer. Coupled with these two products would be instant enlargements and one other would be instant movie film. This, too, has already been invented.

Consider the enormous changes in camera technology during the last few years. We have gone from match-needle exposure to automatic cameras with sophisticated exposure systems, such as the Olympus

OM-2 and the Canon AE-1. There are many others. I don't mean to denigrate them by not mentioning their names, but by the time this is published almost all manufacturers will have changed over to the automatic cameras. These cameras save much money for the professional and make his or her life easier. Of course, they also make it easier for the amateur to duplicate the professional's work. The professional must work harder to improve his work to where no one can touch him. But automatic cameras are only the beginning.

Recently the Mars Lander One and Two touched down and sent back to earth some remarkable color photographs of the Martian horizon. These photographs were transmitted by electrical impulse similar to the way our present color television receives color signals. How soon will it be before we carry just the electronic sighting head and transmit the color signals to our receivers back at the studio? These would be transposed and made into the standard color prints. These inventions are not fantasies, they are realities—they exist today but not in a form that we recognize.

What all this means to the professional besides the implication that one should be cautious making long-term investments in processing and camera equipment is that there is an ever-growing need for each photographer to improve his photography and upgrade himself, and to take advantage of new technology as it becomes available. Perhaps more important is the need to be aware *before* these inventions become common. Success is for those who have foresight. Each new invention creates new jobs and new methods of use, but only by those who have the foresight to take advantage of opportunities as they arise.

Silver is on its way out in the manufacture of photographic light-sensitive products. New chemical compounds are in existence today that can be and are used to create color prints. The 3M color printer is on the market. Its early color prints were crude but how long will it be before the prints have full saturation and scale with a minimum of grain?

We take a Xerox, IBM or Savin dry-copier for granted nowadays, yet it was only a few short years ago that these copying systems were invented. How long will it take before all of the above mentioned companies have copiers that will make full-scale color prints? Are you prepared for the impact on your profession? Have you any idea of the ramifications of such technological advances?

It is not enough that you make good photographs with today's technology; you must have some contingency plans for the future, more especially if you're in, say, your 30s. You could reasonably expect to work for another 40 years in photography. Forty years! Can you imagine the changes? Try estimating the impact on your concept of photography as it is now practiced with just the few changes I've mentioned that *now* exist and probably will be marketable within five years.

No, not all of your equipment will be obsolete, but *you* might very well be—unless you plan ahead.

If what I say is true, and I feel I haven't really scratched the surface, then we had all better be ever wary and read constantly, improve whenever we can, and be ready to make changes as new technology demands.

One last thought: don't buy too much at one time.

Everything I have bought in the last few years is already obsolete, and the changes are accelerating. I find that camera technology changes about every six months, so if you buy, buy cheaply and well, but if you invest, invest in your mind. The creative image is one product that will never become obsolete.

# 31 What Makes a Professional Successful

I've been teaching professional photography since 1972. Most of my professional students had had some experience before joining one of my workshops, and yet only a few were what I'd call successful. Out of the 150 people who have attended these workshops only a handful will go beyond ordinary success and become great. In looking back over my notes on each student I've begun to see a pattern develop. I have almost enough information for a demographic study on what constitutes a successful photographer.

The characteristics are interesting. One common idea surfaced early—that their gross sales had nothing to do with their concept of "success." The amount of money anyone grossed was completely amount of money anyone grossed was completely disregarded as a criterion. The number of their employees was also disregarded as was the size of their studio. Another criterion not considered was "name" clients. So much for some negative considerations.

On the positive side most photographers who had ability were considered successful by the professional students. That is, high quality photography rates high. By high quality photography I don't mean photography showing merely a high degree of technical ability. Successful photographs, accepted as such by advertising agencies and the like, were characterized as having or showing technical ability as a matter of course, but something more must be apparent. And that would be an imagination that showed a talent for seeing. Perhaps even more important was the criterion that the photograph should show the stamp of the maker. I'm reminded of Calvin Tompkins' definition of an artist: "One who gives meaning and interpretation to reality by imposing upon it his own imaginative order."

I look for an *intended* photograph as opposed to a *found* photograph. Not that the found photograph doesn't have meaning and usefulness. This might be called *concept.* All too often though, when I visit a gallery I see photographs with intellectual statements attached, and I get the feeling that the statements were made after the photographs were taken.

Success from a business point of view is generally characterized in the personality of the photographer. I see this in my workshops. The aggressive, curious, even "pushy" photographers are bound to be more successful than the creative types with much ability. A successful photographer is a successful person—period. He'd be considered successful no matter what he did. This type of person is generally more energetic, curious, aggressive, aware and undaunted by small setbacks. He's usually thirsty for knowledge and is a great experimenter. Such people usually take enormous calculated risks in the performance of their business.

In fact, *all* successful people take enormous risks, and running a small business is decidedly risky. But what do we mean by "risks?"

To a photographer, business risk means is he going to do enough business to pay the business bills and have enough left over to support him and his family? That's a broad definition since it doesn't define the business bills; and how much is support and how well does he want his family to live? In the 40 years that I've been a photographer I've seen thousands of photographers who have been satisfied with a lower station in life, with nowhere near the money they could earn if they would but get a traditional job. But they *must* be photographers so they accept a less expensive way of life in order to be what they want to be.

I'm not criticizing; I know full well where they come from. For many years I was such a person myself. In 1948 I left employment at Eastman Kodak where I was assured of a life-long secure position, for the vagaries of the small town studio photographer. For the last 20 years I've been successful, but I will never have the old age security provided by the Kodak Company. Nor will most professional photographers gain such security. This is the risk we take in order to live as we wish—as independent professional photographers.

We accept the risk of having no company retirement plan in favor of the thrill of doing what we like best. The happiness of being a working photographer outweighs the security of a company retirement policy. This is an acceptable risk. Being able to do what you want to do when you want to do it is worth all the money in the world. So we live a little less securely in terms of our finances.

Often professional photographers striving for success will buy a piece of equipment they've seen a famous or successful photographer use in the hopes of emulating him or her. Of course equipment doesn't make the photographer, yet much equipment is sold that way. This is the corollary of copying the technique. Photographers want to know what technique was used to make such and such a photograph. Essentially this is how and why photographic magazines enjoy such a large readership. They're how-to magazines. Anyone writing a book on photography is warned against "coffee table" book or books of pretty pictures—they simply don't sell as well as the how-to variety. The theory is that if you know the trick the photographer used, you can make just as good a photograph as he can. Nothing could be further from the truth.

Why beginning photographers assume that great photographs are made with equipment or techniques, I don't know. Every great photograph has a great deal of long previous mental agitation as an ingredient; every great photo has evolved from a history during which each previous image made by the photographer was refined by the process of trial and error. A mixture of techniques—but small dependence on equipment—much imagination, and an

enormous dose of one most important element—
"chance." These ingredients have made my best
photographs.

This is what success is, at least to me. A superior,
technically excellent, imaginative photograph
evolved from a simple beginning. And, of course, the
sale of such a photograph. As Calvin Tompkins
wrote, a successful photograph is one that has meaning and reality imposed upon it by the maker from
*his own imaginative order,* even if success does
mean different things to different photographers.

# PART 3
## Technique

# 32 Basic Camera Techniques

This advice is for the amateur, beginning professional and the established professional photographer alike and is meant to redefine some basics that are pertinent to creative illustration. Much of this advice is quite simple, and yet many photographers lose sight of these principles.

The exposure on the film is controlled by two factors: the *amount* of light let into the camera to reach the film and the *time* this amount of light is let into the camera to reach the film. The *amount* of light is controlled by the *diaphragm* opening, which can be adjusted by a lever that closes and opens the blades. The diaphragm is marked in a figure that represents the number of times the diameter of the opening will divide into the focal length of the lens. As an example, a lens "stop" marked "f2" on a 50mm lens has a diameter of 25mm, or about 1 inch. If you divide 50mm by 25mm the quotient is 2—this is your lens or aperture stop. The 50mm is the focal length divided by the diameter of the opening in the diaphragm, which is 25mm. Each marking of the aperture, although not arithmetic in the sense that the markings don't *appear* to double or halve, is in fact either twice as large or half as large as the nearest other aperture. This means that moving the aperture lever one stop to the right or left of a given stop either halves or doubles the *amount of light* let into the camera.

The shutter speed dial is obviously marked in arithmetic progression, but for the economy of space, the "1" which would signify the fraction is eliminated, i.e., ½ means one second, ½ means a half of one second, ¼ means a quarter of one second, and so on, right on to ½₀₀₀, which means one two-thousandth of one second. Get into your mind the concept that ¼ is twice as much *time* as ⅛, and that ½₀ is half as much as ½₀.

These two factors control the light that exposes the film, but there must be a combination of one set; that is, one shutter speed and one aperture stop or lens opening. Which set you use for a given film and a given light condition is dependent upon your judgment. Sometimes the subject may dictate which combination you use.

If you use an exposure meter outdoors for, say, a color film with an ASA (speed rating) of 200, you might find your meter showing a number of combinations. You will find ½₀₀ at f16 or ¼₅₀ at f22, and a few more. Which do you use? First, let's call these combinations *parallel pairs.* The point is that for any given film or lighting condition there are many combinations of shutter speed and lens stop, each of which will expose the density of the film identically but will produce a different effect on the type and quality of the image. This is a *creative choice* requiring a subjective decision by the photographer. The slower the film, the more options—parallel pairs—the photographer has to work with. By using a neutral density filter, the options can be increased with the higher-speed films.

A couple of rather simple examples may help to clarify this point. A high-speed action shot of a motorcycle racer would require a high shutter speed of, say, $\frac{1}{1000}$ of a second to "stop" the action, or else the subject would be blurred. An additional effect working for the photographer is that the high shutter speed coupled with a wide-open aperture combination would give much "separation"; that is, separate the cyclist from the background to make him stand out more and focus the viewer's attention on him. A distracting background of the stands with people and other cyclists would be wiped smooth by these two effects. Conversely, at the same racetrack, you may photograph the race cars at the "Christmas tree," or starting lights. Here you might use a slow shutter speed of, say, $\frac{1}{60}$ of a second and couple that to the parallel pair aperture of f22. Now the effect is one of extreme sharpness and detail throughout the photograph. Here there is a greater responsibility on the photographer to compose, since all elements are visible. The exposure of the film in each case would be identical, but the visual effect would be far different.

The thinking photographer rarely uses the same parallel pair—he makes a creative choice.

For years I've decried the practice of "focusing on" a thing or a person. This practice has created bad habits among photographers. Except for studio-product photography, certain journalistic photography and the wedding and portrait fields, I see no need for this type of focusing. The photographic illustrator must use another system. Some older photographers know it as "hyperfocal distance" focusing; I call it "aerial focusing" because the exact point focused upon can be a vague point in the air. Focusing the camera is fraught with misconceptions. Few illustrators focus "on" a subject; they use aerial focusing with the 50mm and shorter focal length lenses. The basic philosophy is this. Unsharp normal- to wide-angle photographs look simply awful, so those lenses are usually stopped down for maximum detail. Conversely, lenses longer than 50mm have little depth, and in the case of telephotos, almost none. So stopping down is useless.

Translating this into action, illustrators use the depth of field scales engraved on all wide to normal lenses. They place the aperture, say f16, opposite the farthest point focused upon. In a board room for an annual report, this could be 20 feet. In a large office area for the same annual report, this might be 50 feet. On a 28mm wide-angle lens, this means that the close-focused f16 would be opposite 2½ feet. The depth then is between 2½ and 50 feet. This lets the photographer concentrate on moving around and "seeing" rather than playing with his camera, looking for scales, and so forth. I usually fix the focusing mount with a piece of tape, moving it as I go from area to area. This depth varies according to the lens I'm using and to the size of the room. But I spend little time focusing, since everything from 2½ to 50 feet is *reasonably* sharp. The amount of depth will vary only slightly from camera brand to camera brand.

Most modern cameras focus "wide open," meaning at f1.8 or whatever lens is being used. This is a false image, since if you are taking photographs at, say, f16, what you're seeing in the lens, you aren't getting on the film. You would have to press the "preview" lever, button or whatever. As soon as you press the release button on your camera the lens aperture drops to whatever you preselected, giving you a much different photograph from what you saw in the viewfinder. Of course, you can press the preview selector and the lens will stop down, but you'll find the image so dark and grainy as to be useless to make a judgment with. So the viewfinder presents a false image in a sense. The creative photographic illustrator learns to focus by scale and mentally makes a visual jump to the f16 image.

From an artistic point of view, photographs look better if the eye is led into the picture. Most photographers try to arrange the subject so there is a nearby object in focus to lead the eye into the depths of the photograph rather than having everything lined up against a wall to be "shot."

Aerial focusing is best achieved with short focal length lenses, normal- to wide-angle, with the smaller apertures increasing the depth as does a greater distance focused upon. Some cameras use colored dots to denote f stop numerals; stay away from them, as you can't see them in dimly lit interiors. Some cameras omit many of the f stops. These are usually the faster normal lenses. You should be using a wide normal or wide angle lens for this work so the high f stop is not necessary. Many of us black out the meters scale, as two scales are confusing, but this is a matter of personal preference.

To sum up, place the smallest aperture (f16) opposite the farthest distance visible on one side of the lens barrel and see where the opposite f16 falls. It will probably be at around three feet. Fix the barrel with a piece of black tape and take all photographs within the two limits. Naturally, you've first figured the proper shutter speed to match the f stop.

# 33 Format Comparisons

In understanding the "why" of buying one camera system over another, you, the photographer, have to consider first just what kind of work you are going to perform. If you are interested in, for instance, still lifes for ads or architectural photography, you most likely need a view camera with the related equipment. If you were a small studio operator responding to all sorts of requests, you most likely would buy a 6 × 7 or 6 × 6 system; the journalist buys the 35mm camera and the related lenses. It would appear that choice depends on mobility and that size has therefore become the overriding consideration. This is a fallacy believed by many.

As a photo-graphic illustrator, I use the *optical*

*effects* of lenses and cameras to produce *saleable images.* This statement is vital to understanding why I use the 35mm. The effects achieved with the 35mm camera and related equipment simply cannot be duplicated with any other camera size or format. That's a flat declaration—I mean it to be.

For instance, one effect spelled out in our discussion of lenses is the "wiping out" or "smoothing" of the background coupled with the extreme "isolation" of the subject. Now if you look at the means to get the effect, you will see that I mention a telephoto of, say, 250mm plus two inches of extension tubes plus a 2X Tele-Extender. The visual effect on *film* (not in the viewfinder) cannot be duplicated with, say, a 6 × 7 camera, telephoto, extension tubes and 2X Tele-Extender. It's close but not quite exact. Another example would be to try to come near the effect with a 8 × 10 or even a 4 × 5 camera. For instance, take a relatively small telephoto lens for a 35mm camera, say a 135mm lens. Now that's not very big, is it? The optical effect duplicated on a 6 × 6 camera would have to be a 220mm lens. Well, that's not so bad, but on a 4 × 5 the lens would have to be 500mm long! And on an 8 × 10 camera to duplicate the effect of a 135mm lens on a 35mm camera, the lens would have to be 4,000mm! No such lens exists but if it did, it would be 158 inches, or about thirteen feet long! For an f8 aperture, the diameter of the lense would be about 21 inches. Think of that and remember that the effects used with the set-up I mentioned require the lens to be opened to f3.5. Now we're getting ridiculous. Even the 6 × 7 can't really come near, since a 260mm lens would be needed to duplicate the effect of a 135mm lens on a 35mm camera. When I suggest using a 220mm Zoom with a 2X Tele-Extender, the effective focal length becomes 440mm. You'd have to have a 500mm lens with the 2X Tele-Extender to come close to the effect. Have you seen Pentax's 600mm lens with the f4 opening? It's eight inches in diameter. Anyway, the larger cameras have their uses and for many purposes the 35mm camera can't come near them. The main thing is that creative images are hard to make, but the effects are best achieved with the 35mm system.

Even the shutter has much to do with creative imaging. In discussing the focal plane shutter, I've mentioned its effect on the image. Special pans, blurs and slow shutter movements are necessary techniques for the creative illustrator. While some 6 × 6 and 6 × 7 cameras do have a focal plane shutter, they do not have the other characteristics.

It used to be that many photographers were overly concerned with grain and the quality of the reproduction. That makes sense for documentary and other types of photography where fine grain is essential, but not in creative imaging. Grain is often sought! I have to use grained texture screens to create some images I need. Some of my most saleable photographs are blowups through a microscope. The grain is an imitation of Seurat and his pointillism. (See the chapter on this technique in my book, *Creative Color Photography.*)

I haven't mentioned, of course, the ease of handling, the weight and the cost problems of using the larger systems. These factors, it seems to me, are self-evident.

# 34 Lenses–Wide, Normal and Telephoto

It used to be thought, and perhaps sometimes it still is, that a wide-angle lens is used to photograph in cramped areas where you can't back up, and telephoto lenses were used to bring something closer for a bigger image from a greater distance. These uses are still valid but bypass the *creative use.* For instance, the imaginative photographer uses the *drawing* characteristic of the wide-angle lens—its ability to reverse the scale and lead the eye into the center of the photograph; this means an ability to arrange the subject material for impact, visually stimulating the viewer by the near-far relationship and the extreme depth of focus. The large foreground object and the small, almost tiny background object, both extremely sharp, are attention-getting—a visual pleasure.

Wide-angle lenses on a 35mm camera need to be about 21mm. A 28mm is not much more than a wide normal and too close in imaging to the normal. A 24mm is a good wide angle for annual reports, where people might be viewed or photographed. The wider the lens the more facial distortion there is, so people must be carefully placed in the center. Even then, although the shapes of the heads are not distorted, they are "fattened" somewhat. Faces on the edge of the frame tend to be completely distorted. But for illustrations of scenes and objects, the 21mm, a high quality lens with no barrel distortion, is the best one to buy. It must be carefully held so that verticals don't bend or curve. Some photographers use bubble-levels that screw into the cable-release socket, but if you're holding the camera to your eye, this does not work well. This is especially true with vertically held cameras. Since most of the images I make are vertical simply because that's what's required by most magazines, I can't use a bubble-level. I find a tripod difficult to use with a wide-angle lens, also, since I need minute adjustments to keep the straight lines straight.

The 21mm has its drawbacks, also: lens shades are almost impossible to fit properly without vignetting. Only one filter at a time can be used and it must be of the proper thread size or else it, too, will vignette. The lens is very sensitive to scratching because its front element is so far forward and the rear element is also exposed and must be capped. I recommend the screw-in type metal lens cap if you don't leave a Skylight 1B on the camera at all times.

Lenses of 18mm or 16mm get to be too gimmicky. They do create some startling imagery, but I think the 21mm or thereabouts (give or take a mm) is the best compromise.

Vertical images have more of the effect than horizontal. I've not been impressed with horizontal extreme wide-angle photographs. Someone who just purchases a 21mm should go out and try a roll of vertical images with a near-far relationship. Naturally, the f stop must be fixed at f22 for maximum depth of focus. Start by finding a small object like a beetle, a flower, or a piece of written material for the foreground, and then arrange one or more of these items on the ground, on a rock or on a fence so that the background is massive or related in some way. I usually carry a box of small objects in the car for this purpose. Practice taking photographs of daisies with something in the background. Try a bunch of cheap dime-store rings.

Motion shots with the wide-angle are very attractive. Pan at a slow shutter speed opposite to the direction of the focal plane travel. If the shutter goes from left to right, you pan from right to left. If you pan with the shutter, the picture will be too distorted to use. A pan with a slow shutter and a 21mm wide-angle is a photographic joy to behold. For inspiration, you might study the paintings of Benton, especially his *July Hay;* examine also the paintings of Munch, in particular *Anxiety.* Brueghel's *Wedding Feast* and, finally, Degas' *The Glass Of Absinthe* will provide additional inspiration. Such study has enormous rewards for the photographer. These painters use perspective similar to that of a 21mm wide-angle photograph.

The normal lens approximates the view seen by the eye, and more important, it approximates the view seen by most amateur cameras; for that reason, I stay away from it. I do use it to hang attachments on. I can see that a journalist might need it for low light levels, but for the illustrator, it's really unnecessary. If I need a repeater, for example (Spiratone), or other prism-type lens attachments, I must have the normal lens to hang them on. The fisheye *must* be used on the normal lens as an attachment unless you have fisheye prime lenses. These are useful but, again, they are crutches for the inept photographer and should be used only for the precise image that calls for it.

The telephoto is much the reverse of the wide-angle lens. I generally fix the aperture wide open. The telephoto has some rather astonishing images to offer—separation of tones and isolation of subject are the most important attributes of this lens. Separation is achieved by the characteristic of the lens to blur all but the subject. Even the subject must be "narrow," since the depth of focus is so limited. But this is its biggest advantage. Sometimes I enhance even this characteristic by putting an extension tube between the body and the telephoto. Less depth and more separation is the result. A 2X Tele-Extender added to this makes the effect even more startling. At this stage, the background, which could very easily be distracting, "smooths" out just as if it were painted. The creative telephoto illustrator must use this characteristic and be able to "paint" the background with at least three colors from where he stands! Sounds odd, but if the photographer kneels, the background can become bluish (sky) or brownish (trees, sticks or woods) or whatever colors are in the background. They become blended. Your artistic palette is limited only by the scope of your imagination.

# 35 Extension Tubes and Tele-Extenders

Photography is fraught with misconceptions regarding the uses of equipment, including the lowly extension tube. Originally a device to increase the image size of the object in macro, or close-up, photography, its real uses have been largely bypassed. There's a *creative use* for these mechanical light pipes that can extend the range of your vision. The tubes are attached to the camera body in place of the lens with the lens attached to the tube. In practice the combination allows you to focus closer when using normal lenses, thus achieving greater image size. But for the illustrator, the tube, when set between the camera and a long telephoto lens, opens up a field of images not generally seen or considered. The more

215

tubes added between the two, the larger the image size and closer the focus. (To keep the focus out, or away, I increase the length of the telephoto with a tele-extender, but more about that later.)

One strange effect of the extension tubes is the size increase of distant objects, which are blurred unless they're bright, in which case they suddenly sharpen due to the intensity of the light. A large image of the sun is made this way. An extension tube of, say, 25mm or one inch, with a 135mm telephoto lens triples the size of the sun over the straight telephoto. The actual sharp focal point may be seven feet, but the sun, being bright, will "burn" its own image into the frame and will appear as sharp.

Extension tubes are rarely used with wide-angle lenses, since they destroy the use of the wide-angle lens and you gain nothing that you couldn't have achieved with a normal or slightly long lens. Tubes usually come in three sizes; a set contains something like a 7mm, a 14mm, and a 25mm. I often use all of them with a long telephoto lens, say around 220mm, with a tele-extender. This combination will photograph an insect as if it were one inch from the lens, but you can stand back from the subject about five feet. I have a photograph of grasshopper eating a blade of a sunflower and I can even see its teeth marks on the sunflower and can see it watching me, yet I was five feet away! If I had tried to get closer for the same type of live shot with just a macro-zoom, it would have flown away.

Extention tubes are vital to the photographic artist. Whenever I have to "paint out" a background, I use the tubes with the tele-extender. This smoothing is sometimes the only way to clear the background of distracting subject matter. This "painting out" of the background is important in creating images for greeting cards, posters, book jackets and advertisements, for many art directors like to place copy in the smooth area. The ability to overprint is one of the important aspects of making this kind of image.

I can't imagine an industrial photographer working without this tube-tele-extender-telephoto combination. Factories, plant and even offices offer hundreds of wonderful images not visible to the naked eye. I've often photographed a dirty, dark foundry in New England and wondered how I was to make creative images in such black holes—especially in color. Extension tubes, the tele-extender and the telephoto combination can reveal many images, especially when there's some flare and backlighting around.

Small-product photography lends itself to this type of photograph. Almost any small object and some not so small can be used. (I use the old cliché "anything smaller than a breadbox.") Set-ups in the studio, with two lights covered by colored gels and resting on a swatch of wallpaper, will make some of the most exciting images by means of the telephoto, tele-extender and the extension tubes.

You vary the combination—change tubes, with and without the tele-extender and a small telephoto, right on up to using all the tubes, the tele-extender and the largest telephoto lens you can find. There are so many combinations, and yet, each has a slightly different effect. It might be easier for the smaller professional to buy non-automatic tubes, since you're not going to stop down—all these photographs are made wide open. A good macro-zoom lens is an enormous help. The use of a zoom in this type of photography eliminates the need to move back and forth trying to find the focus. Once you put anything between the body and the lens, the focus mount on the lens only changes the size but will not focus the camera. With a zoom lens, the zooming feature becomes the focusing mount. If you buy a zoom, make sure it's at least 70–80mm to 220mm or more. If you add the tele-extender to this, you have a straight 440mm telephoto lens. Add the tubes, and you've got something exciting in imaging. Be sure to buy a *slide* zoom as opposed to a *twist* zoom—they're much easier to use for one thing and you'll need this feature for creating "zoom" photographs.

All photographs taken this way use the fixed wide-open aperture, since any depth gained by stopping down is really negligible. You need the extra exposure to push through the tele-extenders, which take up two stops of exposure; and the tubes, all of them, will take another two stops. So shooting with an f3.5 wide open outdoors with ASA 200 EPD translates to about $\frac{1}{250}$th at f3.5 rather than the normal $\frac{1}{2000}$ at f3.5.

The point of the game is create images using the optical characteristics of the lens, tele-extender, and tubes. The quality of the lens, tubes or whatever, doesn't matter, but the power of the image does.

Factory or plant photography requires the tripod —you may very well be getting into slow exposures. Since the area covered is usually small, two small quartz lights such as the Lowell Tote lights are the best to carry. Make a wire frame about 8 × 10 to carry an 8 × 10 gelatin filter. I usually use magenta, blue, green and, once in a while, yellow. These gels can be purchased from Edmund Scientific of New Jersey, from the S. V. Victor Co., and from the Roscolene Corp. For fill reflection, I use folding vanity mirrors, which are inexpensive, can be purchased in any discount store, are portable and can even be bought on location.

I recommend photographing the client's product in this way. Arrange a tabletop: beneath the product, use sheets of wallpaper about 30 × 30. Extension tubes and the zoom are where the photographs are. Be sure to shoot everything vertically. I find that art directors can use these shots for ads and for covers on annual reports.

You can photograph everything in many different ways just by trying various combinations of tubes, lights and filters. Again, the limits are only the boundaries of imagination and creative drive.

# 36 Why a Focal Plane Shutter

The mechanical shutter set between-the-lenses of some cameras limits what I like to call *creative use.* Since the purpose, at least to me, is to create imaginative images or illustrations rather than to document something in front of the lens, I need to be very much aware of the optical capabilities or "imaging" of a lens rather than of its ability to resolve so many millimeters per inch or accurately record colors without chromatic aberration or other distortion. What I look for are characteristics that appeal to the mind visually and I make no fetish of grain structure or even of the way the lens is made. I suppose that in this day the state of the art is such that most lenses have reached a level of reasonable quality—admittedly a vague characteristic, but I see little reason to spend enormous amounts of money on superior workmanship when the image, which is really what I'm after, may be made with a much less expensive lens. I would hazard a guess that the majority of my *selling* images are highly diffused to begin with. However, I will not accept junk; but then I rarely find really poor quality.

The advantages of shutterless lenses are many: they usually have larger apertures for any given focal length than the between-the-lens shutter. This one feature is enormously desirable since I use the telephoto lens for separation and isolation of the object focused on. This draws attention to the sharp, crisp single item subject, and conversely, it effectively blurs or wipes clean the background, an additional feature. Shuttered lenses do the same of course, but with not quite the same effect, as each stop down brings more detail into view.

Focal plane cameras always have a higher shutter speed, so necessary to arrest the subject in mid-flight, so to speak. Mechanical shutters are limited to $\frac{1}{500}$ of a second as opposed to the focal plane shutter that has $\frac{1}{1000}$ and, on many cameras, a $\frac{1}{2000}$. The higher shutter speed allows greater versatility in the choice of apertures and films as well. A high-speed or even a moderate-speed film can be exposed with the aperture wide open without resorting to, say, neutral density filters. As a commercial pilot with over 40 years experience taking aerial photographs, I dislike taking any at less than a $\frac{1}{1000}$ of a second. All sports or action photographs are visually appealing when the action is crisp.

Long telephoto lenses are used for industrial

photography inside factories, and close focusing is then necessary. The absence of the shutter allows closer focusing before extension tubes are needed. Interesting effects are achieved at the higher shutter speed of $\frac{1}{1000}$ when combined with panning.

Consistent exposure is possible with all lenses since only one shutter controls all. If there is an error, it is the same for all lenses. Focal plane shutters are more accurate than their mechanical brethren, and, at least at the present, automatic exposure control exists on focal plane-shuttered cameras only. This feature is of enormous help to the imager in creative photography and especially so in duping and copying.

The horizontal focal plane shutter traveling across the film horizontally creates interesting effects when combined with panning both left and right and moving the camera in a circle while exposing. Combined with the high shutter speed this is another yet different effect. Lenses without shutters cost less, weigh less, and require less maintenance, repair and adjustment. When a camera is kept clean, it rarely becomes erratic. Slow shutter speeds are easier to control with a focal plane shutter than the mechanical. Many a focal plane camera can operate to as much as 60 seconds where the mechanical shutter is limited to one second. Not a vital point but shutterless lenses use a smaller filter size, making them less expensive and increasing the likelihood that other filters will either fit or can be easily adapted.

Their main drawback, I gather, is that the flash synchronization is limited to about $\frac{1}{90}$ of a second, which increases the ambient light effect. I really

don't find that to be entirely true. For whatever strobe
work I do, I purposely use a slow shutter speed, since
I like a bit of ambient light. If the subject's movement
requires the higher shutter speed, then I do go to the
$\frac{1}{90}$ of a second speed.

# 37 The Unseen World

There's an area of photography that has earned me much income, and more importantly, it has satisfied my creative urges beyond my fondest dreams. In marshaling my thoughts for this writing, I have tried to attach a traditional label to it, searching, perhaps, for reader recognition, but I find I can't put a simple title to this chapter, so I'll try to explain how I create these images, as well as to describe the equipment needed and the pictorial results.

I've long been aware that nature has, in its inimitable way, designed the greatest arrangements of light, color, texture and form, but I've also been aware that nature does not always make these things visible to the naked eye. Parallel to this thought, I've found few photographers who have explored the infinite realm of photographic optics. It's a rare photographer indeed who makes a goodly portion of his or her living creating photographic images that are not generally visible. Macro-photography is a common label but generally applies to those photographs where the image size is equal to, or larger than, the actual size of the object photographed. If you study most manuals on macro-photography, you will again find that the practice is generally used to "document" or "copy" rather than use the optical characteristics of lenses and related paraphernalia to "draw" photographic designs.

Early on in a photographer's learning background he is taught to focus and expose as a basic technique. Astonishingly, few photographers go beyond this basic practice. True, they perfect the technique to serve them as sports photographers, photojournalists, pictorialists, portraitists or commercial photographers, but they rarely complete the enormous jump of committing to memory the visual characteristics of lenses and the image "type" and "quality" of each lens and related accessories.

In my Creative Color Workshops, I've had to wean away many students from basics so fundamental to their background that they resist me as if I had renounced God or attacked Holy Writ. I would assume that in any photographic discipline, the final image would be *the* area of judgment. I find groups of photographers, whom I must label as purists, who profess that to use any aid is to cheat at creating an image. An automatic camera is looked upon by them with disdain. It makes me think of the flashbulb replacing flash powder; the strobe replacing the flashbulb; the single lens reflex camera, replacing the rangefinder camera. Each new technological advance in photographic equipment and optics is resisted by groups who feel that to use an aid is to demean the ability of the photographer as an "artist," when, in fact, the true artist finds ways to use advances to explore limitations or boundaries, to create new and exciting images. New technology should be welcomed and embraced as another creative tool to expand your knowledge and improve the quality of your photographic life.

Very soon 35mm transparency film will be developed inside the camera; soon 4 × 5 sheet film will be developed dry; soon color enlargements will be processed in the easel; soon color light-balancing filters will be enclosed in the lens; soon color balancing of a scene will be "automatic"; soon videotape may be used in 35mm cameras; soon television sets can produce an 8 × 10 color print of the image on the tube; soon holography and other types of three-dimensional photography will be common; soon color papers will be on resin-coated opaque or transparent backing. And so on, to infinity. All one has to do is to look back to get an idea of how far forward we're going.

One area that stimulates me constantly is the optical imagery of a macro-zoom lens with a tele-extender and a full set of extension tubes on an automatic 35mm camera. I can't count how much work I've sold from this one set-up. For those who want specifics, I use the Olympus OM-2 camera, because with all the optical accessories, a hand-held meter would be out of the question and the match-needle would be too slow for all but tripod work. The lens is a macro-zoom 70–220mm slide, not twist, zoom for reasons you'll see later; a 2X tele-extender, not a 3X (which is not high enough quality), and a set of extension tubes containing a 7mm, a 14mm and a 25mm. The tele-extender is always attached to the lens; the tubes, all of them, are attached to the camera and to the tele-extender. This one set-up enables me to work from a full *20 feet to 1 inch* without removing or altering any of the attachments. The range of focus from 1 inch to 20 feet is accomplished by simply moving the sliding zoom, since once extension tubes are inserted between a lens and the camera body, the focusing ring is useful only for changing size.

What is most important is that any or all of the images are unique and exquisitely different from anything else in photography. A macro-lens on a 35mm won't even begin to create these exciting images, nor will a macro-zoom alone do it either. Leaving off the 2X extender doesn't work, and if you leave off the tubes, you can't duplicate the images. The set-up has to be as I've designed it. Add an automatic Olympus and the new ASA 400 Ektachrome and you can throw away the tripod for many images.

I often use a polarizer with the above to give me some of the most astonishing colors—rich colors with deep saturation. And for photographing a bee, a grasshopper or a butterfly, you can stand back four feet and fill the frame without the insect flying away. Your backgrounds with this rig have that smooth, creamy color that art directors love to put their headlines on; or the sentiment of a greeting card. A simple change of position and you can change the background color at will. Bend down for the blue sky and place the brick house behind the flower for a creamy red with no definition to mar the quality. A blade of grass six inches behind becomes a tonal column gently curving and adding a design to your dandelion. Add a silhouette of a squirrel lending shape and identification to the natural surroundings. I can never extoll the pleasures of such images without feeling the wonderful thrill of discovery. After 50 years of photography I still become a little boy discovering his first butterfly every time I go out for an afternoon with the camera set up this way.

Those of you who do annual reports or industrial brochures, if you haven't used this rig in a plant you don't know what you're missing. For that matter, neither does the client. I've made countless report covers of an electronic chip, a resistor, or some piece of a product. The designs are endless. To walk through an industrial plant with this rig is to walk through a veritable garden of colorful images.

Indoor lighting is no problem with such a rig. Any thyristor flash will automatically adjust, and at any distance since the lens stop is *always* wide open. So many of the outdoor-indoor images use reflected light from back lighting that you have to use the aperture wide open or else you show the hexagonal blades of the aperture. In fact, I look for those little balls of light caused by backlighting. In industrial photography where I'm setting up a blue and red, or a yellow or green lamp behind the object and bouncing the light and color back into a small product with a series of mirror compacts, I find that these balls of colored light are a must.

The size of the image at 20 feet is about that of an 11 × 14 and at one inch, about the size of a penny. For a walk in a strange and exciting world of color, shape and form, may I suggest the macro-zoom 70–220mm, with a good quality 2X tele-extender and close to two inches of extension tubes.

# 38 The Importance of Duping

1. You need a flat-field lens at the short distances used in copying, so you should use either an enlarging lens, reverse your camera lens, or buy a macro-lens —the macro is the best choice. Many professionals buy their cameras with the 50mm macro instead of the normal 50mm since it is quite acceptable for normal purposes but doesn't have the high f-stop opening. If you're not working in low light levels, this might be the best lens to buy.

2. Whatever lens you use, it must be stopped down two stops to bring the sharpness out to the edges and to give you sufficient depth of focus to cover the thickness of an assemblage of two or even more transparencies.

3. Kodak Ektachrome Slide Duplicating Film #5071 is a magnificent duping film that is low in contrast, full scaled and fine grained, which exposes best with a dichroic filtered light source. This means that strobe flashing duplicating machines are not necessary. The head of any dichroic head enlarger is more than satisfactory. However, try to get one that has an infrared cut-off filter in it. This would mean any number of heads such as Omega, Vivitar and Pentax. A slide copier attachment is really not satisfactory; shuffling filters to a changing daylight is not my idea of precision production. Quartz lights are not a happy compromise either since the heat will cause buckling due to the long exposure. Ektachrome 5071 has an ASA of 9; and duping assemblages with the lens stopped down two stops and the relatively low light level of an enlarger head means exposures can go as high as 60 seconds. Heat will build up in all enlargers except the Vivitar VI with the light pipe.

4. Match-needle cameras can be used but they're awkward and time consuming, so I suggest an automatic camera that will go to 60 seconds at ASA 12—I know of only one at the time of this writing—the Olympus OM-2. (Although the ASA of the film is 9, most cameras use 12 as the lowest ASA. This discrepancy doesn't affect the copy.) However, read your instruction book for your camera's exposure limits.

5. Whatever bellows you use should have *two* moveable standards and a separate monorail track for the bellows to move on. Although you can work with any bellows, focus is controlled by the rear standard, size by the front standard. For ease of operation this type of bellows is best—otherwise you must

move the camera and bellows to focus, which can be very awkward.

6. Turn the room lights out when copying; even a slight glare on the surface of the slide will cause a reflection. I use a Gepe plastic mount and turn the dark gray side up towards the lens. Spiratone plastic mounts work well, too.

7. A motor drive or winder sure makes fun out of drudgery, but if you don't have one, a cable release will do. Pushing the release button won't do at all. My bellows (Olympus) also has the feature of automatically stopping down the lens. Most good bellows do.

Cleanliness is next to Godliness in duping. This can easily be the single biggest problem in duping. Keep a bottle of Edwal No-Scratch handy and de-ionize the dust, then blow it away or wipe the assemblage with a Static master brush.

The equipment and procedures mentioned make consistently good duplicates every time you are when using assemblages. Single dupes are often improved but not originals that contain much sky, water, snow, sand or other clear areas. Contrast increases when you dupe. This works to your advantage with assemblages since the combining of two or more transparencies tends to lessen the inherent contrast. An assemblage might very well look muddy and dark, but, when duplicated, the colors come to life. You have to make that mental jump from what you see to what you know it will look like after duplicating.

# 39 Metering Techniques

**W**ithout a doubt, metering, or finding the correct exposure, is the most perverse problem in photography. With the enormous cost of film and processing it behooves the photographer to cope with this difficulty. The difficulty is really negligible with outdoor photography since the instruction sheet accompanying the film, with all its generalities, is quite adequate for most situations. The barrier lies in exposures under 1/30 of a second and in such low light levels as copying, tabletops, commercial product photography and ambient-lit interiors and, of course, outdoor situations in shadow and shade.

The density of exposed and processed emulsion giving a black and white negative is considered correctly exposed when the density translates to the neutral 18 percent gray color or if in color as, say, a transparency, when the level of exposure is such that if the colors were transformed into gray the exposure would match an 18 percent gray color card. Most meters are color blind and render colors as shades of gray. All camera meters as well as separate meters try to adjust exposure to this one standard. This is why studios use the standard gray card.

The ubiquitous 35mm single lens reflex uses a reflection type meter also programmed to the 18 percent gray card standard. This is why, when exposing color film of colored subjects, the camera meter often lies. Try to photograph a 30 × 40 black card inside under a 3200K 1,000watt quartz light about five feet away shining into an umbrella. The meter will give you a match-needle reading or automatic reading depending on the type of camera. Now change the card to a solid red and then to a white. The three readings will vary. If you exposed negative film black and white all three negatives would develop to a neutral 18 percent gray. Since the meter doesn't know what you put in front of it, it tried to bring everything to a standard gray.

If you placed an incident light meter dead center on the black card the red card and the white card with the domed receptor aimed at the camera, you'd get one reading for all since you're reading *incident* light that is not reflected. Now each developed negative would look different. The negative of the black card would be thin (to print black), the red card would be about 18 percent gray to print normal and the negative of the white card would look thick or dark and print light or what you wanted—white.

If you went through this last part with color transparency film you'd find that the consistent single exposure based on the incident light would render three perfect transparencies, one black, one red and one white. But, if you used the camera reflectance meter, the black transparency would be overexposed, the red about right and the white a muddy-gray.

If you want to beat the meter, carry a small gray card in your pocket and, with a telephoto lens on the camera, hold the card in front of the lens and measure the reflectance off this card for a correct idea of the incident light. I do this in snow, in the mountains, on the beach, in water or in any highly spectacular situations that might fool the meter into cutting down on the exposure too much. You might find you need three hands to do this, but since you don't need to focus the gray card, just fill the frame. You can set the camera at the approximate exposure and read the plus or minus and make the adjustment. The automatic camera has a two stop plus and two stop minus override to make all this easier. Cameras are made for the amateur, not for the professional, and all match-needle cameras have a meter sensitivity pattern based on holding the camera horizontally. Ninety percent of the illustrators, including myself, who use the 35mm camera shoot mainly vertically, and we find there's a slightly different reading depending on whether the release button with the right hand is on top or the left hand is topside with the release on the bottom. Make sure you know your meter's pattern. The exposure difference is slight and doesn't matter for most general subjects outdoors, but there are situations where you could be off as much as a stop or even more, ruining a color transparency. Find out where your measuring cells are. For instance, most cells are in one of four positions: on the sides of the eyepiece reading the focusing screen; atop the prism reading overlapping areas; a split prism in the condenser reading the cell in the camera body. These three all suffer from backlight problems through the eyepiece and in some, compensation must be made if you change screens. Few photographers read polarizers accurately. The fourth position has the cell behind a mirror slit and reads direct light.

One camera, the Olympus OM-2, has two blue silicon cells in the body of the camera aimed to read off a patterned screen in front of the film at exposures above ⅟₃₀ of a second and reading the reflection right off the film itself on longer exposures. This renders long exposures possible and makes for extreme accuracy in low light levels. Since the camera is an automatic—aperture preferred—it does have the plus and minus two stop override, a very accurate camera exposure system.

Perfect exposure varies with type of film and type of subject. Color has less latitude than does black and white, yet to expose black and white for a full scale requires just as much attention to tonality as for a pastel photograph or a heavily saturated color poster-type one. On the average, the best exposure would be at the center of the latitude. On black and white negative film, the highlight area appears early at the beginning of the exposure at what is called the "toe" of exposure. The shadow area is the last to appear on the film. This is why when I was a boy my photographer bosses would say: "Expose for the highlights, and develop for the shadows." (This was in reference to black-and-white film.) Translated into color that means overexpose and underdevelop. Although you can print a black and white negative off a few stops, color is ruined unless the exposure is within one stop. When in doubt it is always better to overexpose black and white and underexpose color. In each case the density gives some saturation.

# 40 Supermeter! The Exposure Meter of the Future

A super-exposure meter should have capabilities beyond the accurate measurement of light. Obviously, calculation ability using microprocessor chips to give instant readouts of the problems onto a display screen is desirable, but no modern meter should be limited to pretty images of light emitting diodes (LEDs). Additional information is needed, such as the ability to read all kinds of light including strobe, degrees Kelvin, foot candles, color temperature (in all three colors), and basic enlarging exposure, and, most important, the calculation function should be able to figure such basic problems as bellows draw as it affects exposure, reciprocity of film, and filter factors, at least in a general way. Furthermore, the calculator section must be programmable. If you take the trouble to list all the problems pertaining to exposure both at the camera and in the darkroom exposing photographic films and papers both negative and positive, you will find that most of these are solvable with mathematical calculations. There is sufficient ability in the most elementary calculator to figure all the problems listed above except the reading of white and tricolor light. With the addition of a simple temperature probe this meter could read $\pm$ degree temperature and the pH factor of the solution.

You think that's a lot to ask of a meter? Everything mentioned above can be done today—but using different meters and calculators. Why is this meter—this *super*-meter—necessary?

There was a time not too long ago when film and paper were the least expensive items for the professional photographer. Individual sheets or rolls of film cost but pennies. Paper, too, could be purchased for pennies per sheet. With the advent of color, film and paper prices started their upward spiral. Color paper was fairly cheap until just a few years ago; positive color papers such as Cibachrome and Kodak's 2003 are now listed at $3 for an 11 × 14 sheet. Once photographers were content to make test prints and, in some cases, just waste a print to see the full range of color and overall exposure; today, this is financially unfeasible. A sheet of 4 × 5 Ektachrome lists for $1 and a sheet of 1993 11 × 14 paper lists for $1.75; Cibachrome is $2 a sheet. It's standard practice to "bracket" exposures in a studio; this means three for one or triple the cost. *The waste from improper exposure determination is easily the most expensive part of professional photography.*

My extrapolations of costs through the last 10 years projected into the next five years indicate prices will be double what they are today. Film, paper and chemicals will drive the average photographer to the laboratories, where, incidentally, the biggest share of the photographic business is; but all the laboratories in the world can't help you at the exposure determination—you're on your own. *It's now time for the magic Black Box to make its appearance.*

It's my opinion that the meter manufacturers have been too slow to see a trend developing; they simply don't recognize the need. The present meters are hardly more sophisticated than Don Norwood's 1933 original. Most of the changes during the past 10 years have been in reality nothing more than technological and manufacturing improvements, such as alterations in the measuring cells and solid state circuitry plus some cosmetic styling with LED readouts, which in many ways are a regressive step since, with the older pre-LED meters, a cursory glance at where the light measuring indicating needle lands shows alternate exposure combinations. The early Westons, Gossens, Luna-Pros, Spectras and Minolta Auto-Meters all show much information at a glance that the newer LEDs eliminate.

Measuring light and color is too important and too expensive to be left to "bracketing." We seem to produce some rather fantastic metering systems in cameras such as the blue silicon cell system that measures low light levels right off the film in the Olympus OM-2. Why can't we have that kind of accuracy in meters? I've been a photographer for well over 40 years, and I'm tired of making interminable tests, bracketing and using plain old Kentucky windage on some rather expensive sensitized materials. If it were at all possible, I would call for a strike, a boycott or in some way effect an economic hardship, but of course, that's ludicrous—or is it?

Let's examine some of our *exposure only* needs: First, the basic daylight-ambient-tungsten constant light meter. It should be able to read incident and reflectance and balance them both if necessary, just as the Spectra Combi-II does now. The measurement should be displayed as a "parallel pair" or a sample shutter speed and aperture combination, perhaps in green LEDs with at least two alternate parallel pairs, one on either side of the green and in red colored LEDs. A side image would show the ASA used and the EV number. Years ago I used a Hassleblad camera, and I always enjoyed the way its lens/shutters are set up with EVs and the depth of focus instantly displayed.

A change in the ASA punched on the computer would instantly change the green and red LEDs to reflect the new computations, and punching in filter factors would show two sets of figures; the readout would hold the original but display a correction with perhaps an f prefix (for filter factors).

Second, this meter *must* be able to measure pulsed light such as studio strobes. This isn't too much to ask. True, separate circuitry would be required, but I see no reason why manufacturers should make us buy separate-type meters. They can combine circuitries easily with a chip and a microprocesser. The same display function would be adequate. Another pet peeve of mine is the useless changing of spheres to disks and back again. Manufacturers! Build your disks into your meters.

The third capability in the super-meter would be its ability to measure color balance and give us a readout in either color correction filters or light-balancing filters. They might even have the readouts in yellow or blue LEDs, or at least we'd be able to see instantly if we were too warm or too cool. I'd especially like to be able to read fluorescent lighting with one press of the button.

A fourth capability is a foot-candle meter. Now, every meter is really able to read foot candles; what makes this one so special is the sensitivity range. So I'll set the range. Kodak is adding foot-candle requirements to many of their films; one such is 6121 Ektachrome Duplicating Sheet film. Foot candles make more sense since the measurement for accurate exposure with this film is half-foot candle. I'd like to see a half-inch deflection in the needle or an accurate readout in LEDs. Foot-candle readings also make much sense in the area of sophisticated copying.

The fifth capability would be as an enlarging meter. This is a vital capability especially with such material as Cibachrome and Kodak's 2003 since the waste of a single sheet is unconscionable. Cibachrome, fortunately, needs no color analyzing—for some unaccountable reason the manufacturers of this astonishingly beautiful film paper supplied accurate balances that can be read right off the box. When dialed in on a dichroic head enlarger, the print is right on the money. But finding exposure is another problem.

The sixth and last desirable element would be a sophisticated temperature-measuring probe that could be plugged into the meter-computer or slipped out of a hole in the meter. This probe could also serve as a pH meter, measuring the alkalinity-acidity of the various solutions. Admittedly, this is rarely used but I find I do make occasional checks of my water system.

I mentioned at the outset that the computer section should be programmable. This was for the reason that there are other problems where the combination of a calculator with a display section would prove useful to photographers. One that comes to mind is the splitting of chemical formulas such as making smaller or larger combinations of E-6 from the one-gallon kit for one-shot processing. Another computation might be in still color photography in the studio; figuring lighting ratios, bellows draw, reciprocity and filter factors. Miscalculations must be eliminated if we are to cut down on the waste of expensive film.

Price? Smice! Have you seen some of the prices for tricolor meters? I don't think my super-meter should cost any more than the best of them. Calculators have gone from $400 to $16 in less than three years. LED and quartz watches dropped in price also. I sincerely hope someone pays attention to these needs of ours.

# 41 Light and Lighting

$A$s professional photographers, we're all aware of the importance of light. We understand that photography is based on the reaction of light on film. Although all the technical aspects of photography are important, the handling of light is easily the most important. One isn't a photographer very long before he or she notices that some photographs are better than others; he then starts playing with various types of lamps, reflectors, umbrellas and light boxes. Yet so little is actually known that the handling of lighting becomes a guessing game. He tries all sorts of experiments with lighting but still can't solve the basic problems. Part of the problem is that, for two reasons, you can't experiment with color negative film and send the work out to be printed. Negatives have at least a four stop latitude, which disguises errors, and the laboratory does heavy, corrective spotting, retouching, dodging and burning on the print; so again, the lighting is disguised. The best way to test lighting is with transparency film. Sometimes, with less than one stop to play with, the errors pop out.

The quality and volume of the light must be mixed in such a way as to achieve a reflection from the recorded subject as close to what the original was or improved. But how does one judge this? Exactly what are we looking for? There are so many variables that must be standardized first. Quality and volume are judgmental words and mean little to someone trying to understand lighting, so I'll try to break down some concepts of lighting in the hope that we all might develop a better feeling for it.

The first humans saw things with the first light —the light of the sun. This light came from overhead and in most cases and for most of the time, the light was directional at about a 45 degree angle, with sunrises and sunsets being at a much sharper angle. So evolution has programmed us all to accept what we see as pleasing as far as the lighting is concerned with a light from overhead and at an angle. When fire was born and taken indoors, it was placed on the ground and used for cooking. At about the same time, one torch was taken from the fire and held high in imitation of the sun, for interior light. Examination of early caves bears this out. At first, crevices were used, and later a crude vine bracket was used to hold the torch. As animal and fish oils were found to burn longer, torches were fixed to the walls of the caves. Even in medieval times, oil lamps were hung on brackets in the houses. And so on, down to modern times. Our present-day street lights and indoor lighting fixtures are usually placed above the head, to simulate the outdoor sun. You can prove evolution has programmed us to overhead lighting; watch children telling ghost stories or trying to frighten each other holding the light beneath their faces. Motion pictures and television have long been aware of the value of the underneath light for telegraphing ominous events.

One of the first corrections or alterations to lighting was the shade, which we still use to cut glare and diffuse light. The earliest shades go back to the days of Aristotle. Another change was the reflector, which, in early days, was made of shells. Some are known to have been made of isinglass or mica. Sometimes our ancestors used quartz crystals to cast colored shards of light. Direct lighting was thought to be harsh and unflattering.

Around the time of the early oil lamps, a method was devised to lower the light by controlling the flame—and so the wick was invented. Since then the low light level is identified with romance and drama. Few of Shakespeare's plays are brightly lit. We've come a long way since then—or have we?

What has this to do with photographers and their lighting? Quite a lot really. Summed up, it means that psychologically, we're used to overhead lighting as being "good" and low-angled, low-level lighting as being "bad." Further, that harsh lighting is not to be desired and soft lighting is flattering.

There's still more for us to understand. For instance, the sun is 93,000,000 miles away. In lighting circles the sun is called a "point source," for obvious reasons. We know that light falls off with the square of the distance, which is quite ludicrous when you're talking about the sun—we couldn't walk away 93,000,000 miles to lose two stops of exposure. But what you *must* know is the difference between the sun and indoor lighting. Any tungsten or incandescent lamp will fall off in intensity with the square of the distance. That means that if the f stop at 10 feet from a 1000-watt lamp is f16, if you double the distance to 20 feet, the f stop will be f8, which is obviously different from the situation outdoors.

Because of this fall-off, which isn't visible to the naked eye since the iris adjusts automatically to lower light levels, the photographer has to depend on a meter lest he expose his film without sufficient detail in the shadows. Tungsten lighting is preferred over strobe in still lifes and product photography so the light can be carefully measured to give equal balance to all products in the scene. The general rule is to use tungsten for all subjects that don't move; conversely, use strobe for all that do. But remember, with strobe you can't see exactly what's happening.

In photographing people, direct lighting is rarely used, with one major exception—fashion. Fashion is trendy, and styles in lighting tend to change from year to year. As an example, red-eye is popular right now, yet for years, red-eye was the problem of the amateur—a flaw caused by the flash being too close to the lens and reflecting through the iris to the blood vessels in the back of the eye and out to the camera. Today if you wish to guarantee getting this effect, you use a ring light, but you have to take the photographs in reasonably dim light so that the model's iris is open, causing the red-eye effect when the flash goes off. Another fashion light right now is the large box reflector aimed just about at nose level. This is designed to give an almost shadowless light on the face. The trick is to get rid of the nose shadow. Yet it was only a few years ago when all fashion lighting was close to portrait lighting—the old 45 degree angle main frontal light with a short fill. Nowadays not to be part of the new trend is to be labeled as old-fashioned.

Strobe lighting does stop the action because of the high speed. This is good and bad: good because you don't get the blur of a moving figure; bad because you can't see the actual effect. Even more important, some strobes change their speed when you use different power. This causes some photographs to be bluish, since the higher-speed strobe, say a $\frac{1}{10000}$ of a second, throws the film into reciprocity. The new films don't like short exposures. Yet, almost all the smaller camera strobes operate in the short duration area. The higher the power, the shorter the duration speed. Strobe carries better than tungsten probably because the camera shutter is open much longer than the duration of the flash, so the flash that bounces around a studio is included in the exposure. Many professionals count on this "ambient" flash as a fill. This is especially true with the use of umbrellas.

A short discussion of outdoor light quality may be in order here. Most professionals know most of the next two or three points but it may still be a good review. We know that as the sun rises and sets each day, and that its color alters as we on earth see it. The color temperature at dawn is usually yellowish, perhaps around 3600 Kelvin; as the day progresses and the sun rises, the temperature cools toward a "blue" and reaches 5500K about noon. After the peak of the day, the sun slopes down toward sunset, and again the temperature changes toward the yellow and sets as pure yellow on a clear day. On a hazy day it is more reddish because of water and dirt particles in the atmosphere. Between the hours of ten and about four, the temperature stays pretty well around 5500K and it is at this color temperature that daylight films are made by all manufacturers. In the United States we call 5500K North American Noon, and this is the standard for daylight films.

Tungsten films are balanced for 3200K, a much warmer temperature reflecting the design of the early filament lamps, which were low in voltage and quite yellow or warm. All manufacturers of photographic lamps have standardized all over the world and made their lamps respond to this temperature. So all the films rated as indoor or tungsten films are rated at 3200K, that is, all but one or two; Kodachrome 40 is rated at 3400K. But the difference is miniscule and easily filtered. So studio lamps are pretty well standardized with quartz lamps. The older photofloods are still around, but because the color temperature changes with age, they're not used where a critical color balance is required.

One fallacy is that every photograph should be balanced to the film used. This is not necessarily so. Some sunsets would be ruined if you took out all the red; the yellow perhaps, but not the hot magenta-reds. The interiors of fine old restaurants and homes would be destroyed if blue filtration were added. Critical filtering is best used with products photographed for reproduction.

We see white light, but what's really out there is white light made up of three colors: red, green and blue; that's what we see. What we don't see is the infrared below the red in the spectrum and the ultraviolet beyond the blue. Of the two we don't see, ultraviolet is the villain. Ultraviolet radiation comes from the sun but doesn't reach earth because of the ozone layer, a band of atmospheric particles about 30 miles wide that shields us from the full effect of the ultraviolet radiation. Interestingly, this protection is being destroyed by our own pollution. It used to be thought that a Skylight 1A filter (half U.V.—half infrared) would filter out the U.V. that the film recorded (they film blue). This is no longer true—we need at least a 1B and if we don't do something about pollution you can expect to go to a 1C. (This is not considering the bad effects on us.)

One last item before we leave our discussion of the sun: Heaven knows how many shades of color are out there; perhaps 100,000 shades of reflected light are available. The trouble is we don't have any way of measuring them. They run from a pure white to a jet black or the absence of light. The eye is not the most perfect measuring instrument of these delicate shades but it's the only thing we've got; it can see a small percentage, perhaps 1,000 shades. When we look through the camera, some of those shades are lost and even more are lost because the film can't record all that the lens sees. Maybe a hundred are seen by the lens, and fewer still by the film. The lesson here is that you can't depend on what you see being recorded on film. Tones are dropped when a scene is photographed on color film. Even more tones are dropped when the transparency is screened for half-tone reproduction. You might say that with a 300-line screen about all you could expect is 300 separate tones. But the film won't record even 300 tones. The creative color photographer anticipates this and abstracts the scene in his mind, enhancing some tones with filters and subduing others, just as the painter selects the details he wants in the scene. Without this knowledge of what's happening when you click the shutter, you will often fall far short of your intended mark in your photography. It's right there in front of you. Mount your camera on a tripod and look through it to see the limits of whatever lens you chose; then carefully look at the scene with the naked eye, pick out small details, and then look through the camera. You won't see them! You must learn to draw with the camera.

While we're still talking about the sun and outside lighting, we might look at outdoor exposures of people. The instruction sheet that comes with the film would have you believe that the condition of the sky is the governing factor in outdoor exposure. This may be quite true with scenics but is arguable with portraits or people. The prime consideration is the exposure on the face. As the subject moves and the light changes due to shade or high reflection of buildings, sand, water, or snow, a special reading must be taken with the meter. This is especially true where the subject is out of the sun or backlit or in shadow. I might say here that no one purposely takes a fashion or portrait photograph with the sun full on the model. If you have to shoot in the sun, turn the model around and, using some sort of fill, flash or card, make the photograph. Most photographers look for soft shade; whether on location in the city or in the country, there's always a way. Direct sunlight creates sockets for eyes, harsh shadows and odd facial expressions. Even direct sunlight flash-filled is not always wise. Try for shade against the side of a building as a reflector fill or, if under the trees, use a soft flash fill.

Fashion photos or portraits under trees requires good filtration. Since sunlight streams through the trees and leaves, it picks up the color green, and the shade for a blue sky is blue; add the two together and you have blue-green, which in photography is cyan. To counteract this lest it appear on the model's face, we use the opposite filter—in this case, red. So a CC10 Red is the filter to use. Photographers often neglect this filter, especially those who use negative color films, thinking that the laboratory printer will make the necessary correction. They are wrong to think this. It is true that the printer, you or the lab can make *overall* correction, but why correct everything else in the photograph? Remember that a properly filtered negative or positive is always better than an uncorrected original.

# 42 Light It Right

One of the most difficult aspects of professional photography is lighting, and most of the problems that photographers face are due to their lack of basic understanding of light itself and how it relates to and reacts on color film. The problems are further compounded by the manufacturers of some lighting units who make outrageous claims as to the guide number, covering power, number of flashes per charge or set of batteries and recycling time.

I often check the ad claims against the test reports in the photographic magazines; the trouble is, I can't find the report when I'm reading the ads, and when I'm reading the reports I can't find the ads.

Let's discuss some basic fundamentals of light.

Probably the first and best-known rule is the one that goes something like this: light falls off, or diminishes, from the source with the square of the distance. More simply stated, you should open the aperture two stops when you double the distance. This first rule applies to all kinds of artificial light—strobe, quartz, tungsten or photoflood. It doesn't apply outdoors or indoors with existing light. This is because the source of light, the sun, is 93,000,000 miles away. You can't get twice the distance away to worry about fall-off. This is also the reason why there is no difference in a meter reading taken on, say, two people 10 feet apart. The point source, the sun, is so far away that there is no measurable difference between the amount of light on each of your two subjects.

The principle doesn't apply indoors using existing light because the light usually comes from multiple sources and is usually spread evenly at most distances. Think of classrooms, gymnasiums, convention halls, many offices and even some homes.

You can see this light fall-off effect written on the dial of your small strobe if you own one. At five feet set f16; now look at 10 feet and you will see f8, and at 20 feet you will see f4 or f4.5, depending on the type you have. This same effect or rule applies to your quartz or flood lights as well, but for the moment let's stick to these small strobes that fit on the camera.

These are usually sold with the idea that they are adequate for indoor photographs. Most are, if used with narrow field lenses. Most don't cover wide-angle lenses; most come with a wide-angle attachment that fits over the head and diffuses the light over a larger area, which in turn cuts down the amount of light on the subject.

I don't like these small camera-mounted strobes as a rule. I don't like the lighting effect of one single flash splashing the subject onto the background or the heavy shadows cast by a single light, or the single plane photography, also caused by the single light. The answer is to use supplemental flash in the form of a "fill" light triggered by a slave. The light has to be attached or held by someone. Quite difficult at, say, a wedding. I do use portable flash units, but I find I need the larger powered type because of the shallow depth of field of the smaller units.

If you do buy a smaller unit, or any unit for that matter, ask if you can check it out first. Photograph a blank wall from about 8 or 10 feet and underexpose the transparency. This will show any hot spots. You'll find the corners darker. If they are, the unit is useless. The strobe manufacturer can be expected to say: "If you have lens fall off, it's not the fault of the strobe."

Although there is some truth to this rebuttal, it is only true when you are using a lens stop near the maximum. That's why I suggest the underexposed transparency be exposed at say f16 or f11. At these openings you should not see lens or exposure fall off.

Another and most important test is how many flashes you can get out of one charge or one battery. The instruction book says 80–1,000. Some spread! However, there is a clue there. A spread such as the one mentioned means you have a thyristor unit or a squelching flash. So the only way you can get 1,000 flashes is to take all your photographs at six inches. Since very few do that, the other figure is the one that is important to you, especially if you are doing weddings or annual reports. You need some 80–100 flashes from one charge; I wouldn't settle for less.

*Don't buy a battery unit if a rechargeable unit is available.* As an example, one of the most common batteries used in the median-powered units is the new 510 volt photoflash unit. It lists for $24.50 and can be bought for something like $16.50. They don't last over 100 flashes. If that is a wedding or annual report you're doing, this expense will cut into your profit.

Wedding photographers and annual report and interior photographers use wide-angle lenses rather than the normal ones for their work. Besides the obvious reason that they are often forced to shoot from a cramped position, they use the wide-angle lens to cut down on the amount of flash needed. Ten feet away with a wide-angle lens at, say, f16 would mean f8 at 20 feet shooting with a normal lens. The light is that much farther back.

I made a number of tests with higher-powered units and found that the battery units were useless and expensive, that most of the wide-angle attachments caused hot spots and that the fall-off was horrendous. The guide numbers must have been tested in a white-walled room with white clothes.

My conclusion was that the biggies were better units, albeit they cost more. Ascor, on the other hand, was a very good unit; so was old Hico and, of course, Norman. The Metz 403 and the Braun RL-916 were also excellent.

Lighting large interiors is an art all by itself. I'm an old number 2B flashbulb man myself. Flashbulb training makes some smashingly scrumptious transparencies. But what work! Hiding lamps all over the lot, taping distances, checking for reflections, firing one set of bulbs just for the Polaroids and taping wires so that they are out of sight.

Strobes are harder to use in one way; they don't throw light as far, but they spread it better. They're also not as powerful as flashbulbs. Strobe photography is all right with an umbrella and with the light directly in front of the subject; with different conditions I insist on a fill. Some of my fashion shots are taken with the single light for a "kookie" or "camp" amateur effect similar to the old newspaper photographers' photographs around the 1930s. But you must remember that I have a 50′ × 30′ studio that is all white with a huge 24′ × 12′ curved white background that serves as a reflector. Especially since I use a 2400 WS Tekno Balcar strobe, that unit throws an unbelievable amount of light all over the place, and the white studio and the white background act as a huge reflector.

What this all boils down to is that you need more than one light. You need as much power as you can afford. You should use rechargeables rather than battery. The unit should be capable of at least 80–100 flashes without recharging, all at 10 feet. The recycling time should be no more than 5 seconds, even at the eightieth flash. The head should be able to tilt for bounce flash with the sensor reading the bounce reflected light; the head should be demountable. There should be a provision for a slave unit with a simple triggering device. The watt seconds or the guide number with Vericolor S rated at 80 ASA should be at least 160 as a minimum. The unit should have an AC capability and it shouldn't weigh a ton. I would like to add that it should be inexpensive, but haven't I already been silly enough?

The units I have mentioned comply with all of the above conditions. If you are buying portable strobes for professional photography, go for the best ones; you can't afford to goof for the sake of saving a few dollars. This is one of your main tools. A poor unit will give you a case of hypertension you won't believe.

# 43 Strobe Lighting Techniques

$S$trobe lighting has been around for quite some time. I can remember using an old Sylvania model in 1949. The portable battery box weighed in at twelve pounds, and the early flash reflectors were highly polished chromium and the effect on the subject, whether a model or product, was so bright, glaring and harsh, that too much was revealed. Well, much has happened in the intervening years and technology has improved over Dr. Harold E. Edgerton's first units.

Wedding photographers are the biggest users of the portable units today, with the family amateur following close behind. The units are usually thyristor controlled, meaning automatic, (see chapter 42 for a better description) and they pack quite a wallop. The thing is that the light is raw, and raw light is not flattering to people or to products, so after attempts at reducing the glare with handkerchiefs rubber-banded to the lamp head, the bounce flash was born. Soon, manufacturers made the heads swivel for bouncing off the ceiling. This was fine for horizontal photographs but impossible for verticals. Many photographers opted for the "quick-release" bracket, but a bracket is awkward, since we humans were given but two hands. How do you cock the shutter, transport the film or whatever? So the swivel flash head became popular.

Bouncing light off the ceiling is easier and renders a softer photograph than the straight flash, but it has a couple of drawbacks. The main one is the increased distance the light must travel to the ceiling and thence to the subject. Since light falls off with the square of the distance, you need a pretty high-powered unit or else you'll have little depth. The color of the ceiling suddenly becomes important. Most are white or off-white or beige and are usually flattering. Any other color ceiling, and you must rule out using bounce lighting. If the ceiling is high (more than the standard eight feet found in most homes), the distance the light has to travel is excessive—overpowering small units. Still another consideration is that ceiling bounce lighting causes small disagreeable shadows to appear under the eyes, nose and mouth. One serious problem is the exposure. You must figure the distance to the ceiling, thence to the subject. A rule of thumb is that the distance is increased by one-third for a normal eight-foot ceiling. Having an automatic flash is a great help here, since the sensor on the flash will accurately measure the light on the subject.

*Direct-bounce lighting* has numerous advantages for the professional. But there are so few units available: the Ascor 1600, Braun F-900 and the ubiquitous Vivitar 283 and the 365. The Vivitar was the first to come out, with a rather unique bounce bracket that uses the back or white side of the 18 percent gray card photographers own anyway. This card was fitted into a metal holder, which was attached to the ears of the flash unit. This was a bit awkward, and it took some getting used to, but it sure made lovely, soft flash photographs. The Ascor too has a card system, but the Braun has a folding cloth reflector bracket made of an aluminized lenticular-surfaced cloth that, in my opinion, is the best "look" for a flash—neither too flashy nor too soft. Its most valuable asset, to me, is that it somehow evens the flash out to the point that, with a 21mm lens on the camera, the light is so evenly spread, without hot spots in the foreground or blocked shadows, that the image is as near a flat spread of light as you can get. On a color negative I've taken exposures of foreground objects from 3 to 30 feet in front of the lens with a minimum loss of detail in either the highlights or the shadows.

Carrying one of these around in public might be embarrassing, but I've found not having excellent photographs at the end of an assignment can be more embarrassing. I use this system on annual report photography with a Braun slave F-900 and a similar reflector. This Braun also has a provision for substituting a small umbrella. Although I don't do weddings, I can imagine this could be useful at such occasions, also.

You can make your own bounce reflector out of Reynolds Wrap (the dull side) and a mount board. Simply spray an 11 × 14 card with 3MM Spraymount and lay the Reynolds Wrap on it. Attach this to the flash unit with a bracket made of a wire coat hanger.

Strobes are balanced for 5500K or daylight, of course, but reciprocity failure must be compensated for with these newer units. I use a warming filter for that purpose, a CC10 Red to compensate for the ultraviolet of the short flash duration. I often use that filter on the flash itself, but more about that later.

Flash-fill outside in daylight is so easy and generally understood by all photographers that it hardly bears mentioning here, but for the few who might want to review the technique, I'll hit the high points.

Professional illustrators dislike shooting in direct sunlight. If you're forced by circumstances to shoot in direct sunlight, turn the model around and backlight him or her with the sun and flash-fill. The trick is to get one stop less exposure on the fill than the overall exposure. Using an incident light meter, meter either a gray card for reflectance or aim the meter at the subject for incidence. (Remember, the light is falling on you.) Using this exposure, find your f stop, then, making sure your camera will "synch" at the shutter speed you've chosen, flash-fill one stop less than the exposure you're using. If f16 is the aperture then the fill must be for f22. If you're using an automatic flash unit, it must be set to give the equivalent of one stop less. Flash-fill should be hardly noticeable and shouldn't look "flashy."

*Double-filtered flash lighting* is one technique used by most illustrators, and yet it's not taught anywhere, to my knowledge. The need arises when you're on an annual report assignment and the corporation executive wants to be photographed against the background of the working people or the factory itself. The problem arises from the fact that the large office filled with workers is usually lit by fluorescent fixture lamps or, if in the factory, the lighting could be mercury vapor, fluorescent and daylight. Such lighting in the factory can be agreeably filtered, but it would be unacceptable for a portrait. This means you need a predictable light on the subject (executive) and another filtration for the background.

Obviously the executive should be photographed by strobe flash, but the correction filter over the lens for the factory/plant background would give him or her a reddish look. The answer is to use two filters, one on the camera to correct the background, and an opposite filter on the flash to counteract the camera filter and match the light with the film and the executive.

The film should be Ektachrome or Kodachrome Daylight filtered with an FL-D filter (Fluorescent-Daylight) or a CC60 Magenta—CC20 Red on the camera. That takes care of the background lighting. This, with clear flash, would make his or her skin tone too magenta-red, so you counter this color by placing the opposite filter, in this case, a CC50 Green or a CC50 Cyan, on the flash which depends on the conditions at the plant. I've used both and tend toward the cyan. Because this keeps coming up regularly, I had to buy the Braun F-900 flash to get the right bounce reflector. This unit uses a four-inch gelatin filter. Since I have these for my studio cameras, I've taken to carrying a few four-inchers with me on annual report assignments. The final portrait will result in a well-balanced photograph, although the background might be a shade warm or cool. Reciprocity can cause much trouble with slow shutter speeds with this film, so I try to use nothing longer than a $\frac{1}{10}$ of a second. My favorite for the double-filtered portrait is $\frac{1}{30}$ of a second.

# 44 Copying Techniques Simplified

Copying might not be creative but it certainly takes a lot of technique to do it right. Every photographer has heard the basics, but I'll go over them quickly for those who aren't quite that familiar with them. Let's assume we're going to copy a painting—one without glass over it. We'll hang it on the wall and set up our two lights, one on either side at about a 45 degree angle to the flat plane of the wall. The lights should all be the exact same distance from the dead center of the painting; this can be checked with a tape. The lights are of equal intensity and should be quartz lamps. The wattage is immaterial, but the reflectors should be identical. The camera is on a tripod at dead center for height and dead center laterally. Each light should be about three or more feet away from the painting to be copied and "feathered" to spread the light—that is, turned away from the painting so that it is aiming across to the other light with just a little more angle to the painting; this spreads the light evenly. You can check the distance and balance of the lights by holding a pencil at the exact center of the painting and checking the angle and intensity of the two shadows made by the lights.

So much for the physical set-up. Now you should have two large 12 × 12 polarizing filters, one to fit in a bracket over each light. These filters have to be placed for vertical polarization; you stand at the lamp and, with the filter over your eyes, rotate it until the reflections diminish. Now do the same for the other side, and then place each in its bracket and go to the camera. It matters not whether you're using a 35mm or an 8 × 10 camera—the principle is the same. Hold a polarizing filter over the lens after checking with your eye. You have now eliminated all reflections externally. Of course, you've turned out the room lights. Use a compendium shade on a view camera or a lens hood on the 35mm. Now take a foot-candle reading with a good foot-candle meter such as the Gossen or Photo Research FCM. Run the meter from corner to corner, aiming the flat receptor toward the lens to lessen the cosine effect. The meter needle shouldn't vary more than a quarter stop. Don't use your regular meter with a flat receptor, as the scale deflection is too small. Better just to eyeball it. Now switch to your incident light meter and with the flat side of the meter touching the surface of the painting, aim the receptor at the camera lens and take your reading.

I copy in color, so for sheet film I use the Ekta-chrome Professional tungsten type. With a 6 × 7 roll film camera I use the EPT Ektachrome Professional Tungsten 120. With the 35mm camera I find the best film is Kodakchrome 40, a tungsten type film ASA 40 but it's 3400K, so I use a CC10 Yellow to bring it back to 3200 to match the lamps. Of course you can use any other tungsten-type emulsion, too. I would tend to condense (underexpose) the exposure slightly for saturation. This would be especially true with light sky or water paintings. This technique would hold the detail in the highlights. It would be helpful to know the final use of the transparency. For example, should a poster be made where a large blowup is needed? If so, a really condensed exposure is required. However, if the transparency is to be reproduced one to one, an average, normal density is fine.

If you copy an original that is small, it's best to use a flat-field lens, such as an enlarger or macro-lens. These must be stopped down at least two stops to control the edge sharpness. My rule is to use a copy-stand for an original smaller than 11 × 14, and the wall with the lights for larger than 11 × 14. For small originals I use two 100-watt household bulbs in a gooseneck carrier attached to the copystand post. I use these small powered lamps because the larger lamps give off too much heat at close distances and are difficult to work with. The lamps get hot and the originals will curl, especially if they're sheets of paper or prints. The 100-watt household bulbs give sufficient light through filtration of about ⅛ second at f8. Because these bulbs are so low in Kelvin, I use CC55 Cyan and CC25 Magenta with Kodachrome 40 tungsten film.

I keep an ultraviolet lamp in the darkroom near the copystand, and I check each piece I copy for "whiteners," a bluing put in the mix when the paper is made to whiten the look. This will photograph with a bluish cast and you'll think you goofed in filtering. Not so—if I find a fluorescing, I place a U.V. filter over the lens with the others. For polarizers for the lamps, Spiratone sells a set for about $20 with clips to fit the little aluminum reflectors. I use these but find I don't need the one over the lens with close work. Needless to say I like to do this work with an automatic camera as it reads the variations in the density of the originals and evens the exposures.

It goes without saying that glass and reflecting surfaces cause problems. One can photograph through glass with the system above but there's a slight loss of saturation, so try to take the original out of the frame before copying.

There is a rather simple, yet very effective, way of quickly making colorful slides of typed or drawn material for lectures and titles. Original black and white subjects are placed under the 35mm copy camera on a copystand and illuminated by either the 100-watt bulbs or ordinary photographer's quartz lamps. The film used should be any Ektachrome tungsten film rated at either 50 or 160 ASA but, and this is most important, exposed at either 150 or 500 ASA. The match-needle or automatic feature of your camera will accurately expose the film; however, there must be a color filter over the lens. Any type of filter will do—a green, red, blue, yellow, cyan or whatever, and they need not be pure photographic colors. Even spotlight gelatins make excellent filters for this process. The film is processed as a *negative* even though it is a reversal film. This is the reason for the use of the high ASA.

The results are nothing short of astonishing. All the black lettering or drawing becomes pure white and the background shimmers in vibrant, almost fluorescent, colors exactly the opposite of the color of the filter used over the lens. The film is processed in Kodak's C-41, which any lab will do on special order, or you can do it yourself in Unicolor's K-2 process in 13 minutes. It has taken little time and space to describe this process, yet it is easily a technique the creative photographer should be aware of. This technique is also the way to photograph or copy a 35mm transparency using the colored filter mentioned above. The slide takes on a monochromatic vibrant color where the background was clear and alters all other colors to the opposite. Your creativity is only limited by your imagination and your ability to make the mental visualization.

# 45 Redefining the Element

According to the dictionary, an *element* is a part, component or constituent of a whole. This one of many definitions suits the illustrative photographer well. Almost all illustrations, advertisements, greeting cards, posters, book jackets and skin-packaged items use a number of elements arranged in such a way as to combine into a cohesive whole. Sometimes the element would be a simple overprint of lettering, but more often there's a combination of images. Just in the last five or six years I've noticed more and more advertisement illustrations containing multiple images. Some are so interwoven that it's difficult to tell where one leaves off and the other begins. In others there's no attempt to disguise the use of multi-

270

ple images. Nor should there be. An illustration is complete when it achieves what the maker intended. But whatever assemblages, multiple images or combinations of elements you see, those that work best are those whose larger elements are artfully combined from single elements that are simple and easily recognized *even if they were in outline!* This, more than any other characteristic, especially identifies the element. In photography, and especially in creative illustration, this must be a cardinal rule. Exceptions do come along, but they're rare. Once in awhile a very simple element can be combined with something a little busier and the combination will work. Sometimes three elements will work together, but each of them must be singular, simple and easily recognized even if reduced to a line drawing. The key word here is *recognized.* With those two characteristics in mind one can quickly think of at least 30 elements. Now let's add another characteristic germain to photography and what we're doing with elements; make one or more of the elements *translucent.* Now you have the third characteristic and are ready to begin understanding an assemblage.

Why translucency? Because in the combining of transparencies, one over another in preparation for duplicating, the colors of one are sometimes combined with the colors of the other. Startling effects are created where one transparency uses the color of the other as its background. Visualize the face of a model filling a frame. Except where the eyes and nostrils show more saturated color, the facial area is clear for whatever you wish. If you combined the face transparency with an apple cut in half, his or her face and the half-apple would blend into an illustration. Of course that's an oversimplification of an assemblage, but if you think about your own ideas, you'll soon develop thought paths and start your own creations. The trick is to think in terms of simple objects that have some translucency.

What makes a good element? Almost all parts of the human body that are recognizable by themselves, that is, as if they weren't attached. The ear, eye, nose, hand, foot, face, breast, buttock and the overall shape of the human body are some in that category.

Perhaps the most pertinent and easily the most popular element is the sun. Perhaps because we're a world of sun worshippers, wherever you use the sun, you can be assured of success. Sun-images should be larger than normal and usually deep red in color. Clouds in all shapes and sizes are very popular, as are animal faces and the entire animal. Birds are as popular as the sun, especially seagulls, whose graceful shape enhances all photographs. They're best photographed in flight and with wings outstretched. This thought of soaring brings man-made things to mind; airplanes, helicopters, airliners and parachutes. This in turn brings sports to mind. Almost any sports participant makes a good element, but only if used alone and isolated from a distracting background. Sometimes just the accoutrements of sports: rackets, bats, balls and clubs. All fruits, sometimes whole but often sliced, make excellent elements. The apple is my favorite, again; it is steeped in symbolism. The orange, melon, grapefruit, and other fruit can also make excellent elements. Many printed items make good elements. Think of sheets of music as the most common, but posters and especially wallpaper also are good. Newspapers, boats, trains, cars and parts of them; musical instruments form another category that's popular. Flowers are still liked but have become a photographic cliché—I suggest that the professional stay away from them except where the concept works outstandingly. All textures are more than useful. Photograph cloths, textured card stocks, such as many of the Brainbridge boards. Brick walls and old barns have some of the most commonly used textures and serve many purposes.

The list is potentially endless and is limited only by the boundaries of your imagination. Since the sun is one of the most important of all elements, a short discussion on how to photograph it is in order. The most attractive sunsets occur on slightly hazy or even muggy days, not the clear crisp days you might imagine. Cloudy days are more picturesque. When the atmosphere is heavy with moisture and dirt particles, the sun's rays at sunset are refracted through these particles coloring the sky around the sun with a grainy, purplish color and hazing the sun into a deep magenta-red hue. The point of view should be as near to the perpendicular as possible. You may think that is impossible; that without moving around the earth you couldn't change your point of view. Not so. Approach a sunset from different angles within your own community and you'll see that some angles create an ovalling effect while what you want is the rounder circle. The color is always best when you catch the sun just before sunset. Don't worry about the horizon of trees just below the sun. With the method of photography I suggest, these blur into a dark reddish brown. I sometimes turn the transparency *upside down,* creating a neat dark top for my final photograph! Take your meter readings alongside the sun with no sun in the finder. This is for the match-needle type only. For the automatic camera, you can aim directly into the sun, but you must dial the manual plus/minus wheel to plus two stops! You must extend the exposure because the meter sees the bright sun and thinks: "Oh, oh, gosh that's bright, better cut down the exposure." You have to compensate for that. Using a separate meter that might take in the sun, such as an incident light meter, turn around and meter the area behind you. Use that although it is not as accurate as with an automatic camera.

Your equipment should include an extension tube of about 25mm on the 35mm camera and a 135mm telephoto lens. This is the minimum. It focuses at about seven feet, but no matter; the sun will "burn" its own image and will look sharp. *You must use an 82B filter* for the proper effect. Most sunsets suffer from too much yellow and must be compensated for. However, I'm not out there with you, so I can't make your judgment. Sometimes, especially when you're photographing the sky along with the sun, the gorgeous colors are not yellow, but you'll have to decide that. The sun itself needs correction. You must not close down the aperture, not even one stop, or you'll see the hexagonal shape of the aperture blades reflected in the image. If this causes too much exposure, you'll have to use a neutral density filter to cut down on the exposure.

Be sure to make most photographs *vertical;* you will probably have far fewer buyers for horizontal transparencies.

# 46 Space Perceptions

Humans have been interested in the perception of objects in space at least since we first wondered how a picture or image develops in the human eye. In ancient Greece it was popularly thought that objects were seen because they emit what was imagined to be a continuous series of extremely thin membranes in their own image that fall upon the eye and there merge into the picture that is perceived. Only after long experimental research was a more tenable concept reached, in which space was described in terms of three dimensions or planes: height (vertical plane), width (horizontal plane) and depth (sagital plane). These planes all intersect at right angles, and their single axis of intersection is defined as being

275

located within perceived three-dimensional space, that is, in the eye of the perceiving individual. Humans do not ordinarily perceive a binocular space or a separate visual world from each eye; rather, they see a "Cyclopian" space, as if the images from each eye were to fuse to produce a visual field akin to that of the one-eyed giant of Greek mythology.

Photographers who wish to become highly creative and imaginative illustrators would do well to study a relatively new science—that branch of psychology called "space perception." This field concentrates on the factors contributing to the perceptual organization of objects in space, such as cues to depth perception, movement, form, color and their interaction. How one perceives that there are six sides on a cube even though only three of them are directly visible at any one time is known as "amodal perception," and this presents a special problem. Another question involves the effect of the so-called "mirror-ego" on perception. For instance, when one touches one's skin while looking at himself in the mirror, does he experience the touch as if it were in the mirror image or is he perceiving it to be in contact with his own body as it actually appears in the mirror?

Space-perception research has tended to become a distinct specialty of psychology because of indisputable evidence that behavior in this area is involved in orienting the individual to his or her environment. Specifically, man's orientation in space typically seems to reflect strivings such as seeking food and avoiding injury, but we wouldn't have effective orientation behavior unless the environmental information reaching our sense organs were organized to permit objects in space to be perceived at least approximately in a way that corresponds to their physical, or actual, condition. This is called *veridical perception.* Not all perception of space, however, corresponds to reality. A large number of such perceptual effects as optical illusions show space as deviation from reality. A photographer, working in the vertical and horizontal flat planes without the sagital, or depth, plane must be able to separate his optical perceptions, including his own psychological impressions of what he sees, from the reality of the camera. More important, he must be able to translate the image seen through the lens not as a psychological perception, which most photographers now do, but as the "actual" image as it appears on film. This translation must be some sort of a filtering process where the arrangement of objects, as seen through the viewfinder of a single lens reflex, is translated through the filtering process into film images completely devoid of psychological impressions as to color, depth, space, gravity, etc.

In order to do this, the photographer will have to depend upon visual factors in space perception. You might think that perception in space is based exclusively on vision. Yet psychologists are aware that visual space is supplemented perceptually by clearly identifiable cues from auditory (sense of hearing), kinesthetic (sense of bodily movement), olfactory (sense of smell) and gustatory (sense of taste) experience. There are other cues such as spatial cues (sense of balance) and other modes for sensing body orientation. These various "spaces" are not perceptually independent of one another. Experimental evidence shows them to interact in producing unified perceptual experiences.

A photographer, aware that he sees space in "cues," must recognize that the camera isn't able to identify auditory, kinesthetic, gustatory and vestibulary stimuli (sense of balance) since it cannot pick them up. However, a good illustrator can create the impression or illusion of these cues.

The process of perception, especially of depth and distance, depends on information transmitted through the various sense organs. These cues indicate the distance at which the objects in the environment are located from the perceiving individual and from each other. For the perception of the distances of objects located very close by, one depends upon his tactile, or touch, sense.

The psychology of spatial perception is quite involved and is not needed in this chapter for the average photographer, provided that he is aware that when he is viewing through the SLR, the camera does not filter out the other four senses or cues. Only through experience can one look at a scene and previsualize its effect on film when devoid of psychological cues that only distort what actually appears on the film. Photography well studied in such light can build a warehouse of experience. Experience can thus become a conditioned reflex. In fact, all photographs made by respected photographers manifest this reflex, whether or not their makers are aware of it.

Here is a simple example of one such conditioned reflex. You are well aware that the camera has but a single aperture stop with which to make the exposure. This aperture has but one set of depth distances, depending on the focal length of the lens, the distance between the scene or objects and the aperture stop itself. The resultant photograph has greatly increased contrast with tones dropped in the highlights and shadows somewhat blocked even though these same highlights and shadows are visible in the viewfinder. While looking through the viewfinder, the creative photographer mentally abstracts the scene, dropping tones he knows won't show and blocking shadows he knows will be blocked; in effect, he translates the scene onto the film in his mind. This is called "filtering."

If he can add enough of these conditioned reflexes and put them together in various combinations, he will create new envisaged photographs that more nearly represent the intended actual photograph. This means taking advantage of *spatial* impressions and not being fooled by *psychological* cues that cannot be photographed.

Because of its enormous capability, the eye has a tendency to fool a photographer since it can focus anywhere and can open or close its aperture unconsciously, automatically adjusting the diaphragm (iris) when looking at a highlight or shadow. The photographer has to go beyond these cues of accommodation and convergence. The only way the camera can use the cue of accommodation is to have a multiple aperture. The cue of convergence, such as the eye's ability to follow-focus a moving object, will some day be a feature of cameras.

Years ago, there were many attempts to invent three-dimensional cameras, such as the stereo cameras of the 1950s and 1960s. Prints, too, were imitation three-dimensional through lenticular screens laminated onto specially made color prints. You don't hear much about them now, but you will again.

Working photographers can expect one day to find photographic manufacturers making a lenticular tissue that can be mounted onto a color print to create the illusion of three dimensions. Work in this area has been at a standstill for many years, primarily because of the crudity of the system, since one needed special glasses to see the three dimensions and because flat printing wasn't practical unless everyone were to read with stereo glasses.

# 47 What You See Isn't What You Get

Looking through a match-needle single lens reflex camera is about as useful as looking through the old-fashioned rangefinder camera or the wire-finder of an old Graphic, since what you see in the viewfinder hasn't the remotest connection to what actually is seen by the film.

To begin with, your viewfinder shows a lot less area than actually appears on the exposed frame, but that's not really as egregious as some of the other differences between the film and the viewfinder. For instance, most 35mm cameras focus and meter wide open, only closing down to your preselected aperture at the moment of truth, when the shutter is fired. Yet this is, to my mind, the least of the problems of visualization.

Creative photography requires a better understanding of how light affects film than the average photographer has. One can "oh wow" at a colorful scene, and yet the resultant slide seems to be quite different from what was expected. The reason is simple. Think of the sun as being 93,000,000 miles from earth and one huge point source of light with enormous power and brilliance. When it shines on our scene it may very well show as much as 10,000 shades, hues and solid colors as well as numerous textures. The eye, with its marvelous ability to adjust its iris, sees deeply into the darkest of shadows and almost at the same instant, can find elusive detail in the clearest of highlights. This is accomplished by the magic of the optical characteristics of the eye, the optic nerve, and the receptors at the back of the eye. But the camera aperture is set at the whim of the photographer, and where it's set determines much about the visual detail in the resultant transparency. Since the photographer can't see the effect in advance, most photographs are guestimations at best, and more often than not, just another record shot. Part of the reason, maybe a major part, is the fact that the single aperture setting determines which highlights and what detail in the shadows shall appear—a selective option that most photographers not only don't use, but don't know how to use.

Simply stated, increased depth of field (sometimes called depth of focus) increases the perceptible detail just as larger film sizes (e.g., an 8 × 10 transparency) show more details of a scene, size for size, than does a 35mm transparency of the same scene.

Exposure, too, governs whether you see detail in the highlights or the shadows. Increased exposure beyond the so-called normal on transparency material opens the shadow detail and, conversely, decreasing the exposure shows detail in the highlights. Interestingly, picking the exposure is a trade-off.

Regardless of what exposure you pick, the transparency material can't compress all of the 10,000 little shades of color, or even record them. The loss brings the scale down to about 1000 to 1. Quite a loss when you think about it. Prove it to yourself. Look at a scenic view, make a transparency, process it and compare it to the original scene. You may be quite shocked.

Let's continue with this hypothesis. Assume you now have a 4 × 5 transparency and it's now on the light table and you and the art director/client are looking it over. Your eye or his will open to look into the shadows and close when looking at the highlights —*but the engraving camera can't do that!* It has to pick one aperture, so it has to drop more tones. A mask will help, but not many photographers know how or care to make a silver mask, although the devices are quite simple to make.

So the engraver picks one aperture, and he, too, has the same option of dropping highlights or opening shadows. His separations have once again compressed the scale. The printer further reduces the visual impression of detail because he prints onto paper, and some detail is lost between the transparency and the reflective paper.

Let's go back to the camera for a moment. If, when you are looking through the finder, you can visualize just what is happening on film, you can make value judgments that can prevent much distress all along the line. As an example, since you can't see what's happening on film (most preview selectors are so dim at any f stop as to be useless unless you have the eyes of an owl) may I suggest you use a Spectra Color Viewing Filter such as Hollywood directors use? You may not be able to direct two 5000-watt Brutes into the shadows, but you may be able to take a different point of view, one with less contrast between the light and shadow—if this is desirable.

Perhaps I should have mentioned the first and most important option—just don't take a photograph unless the loss of tones is not only acceptable but contrived. I still think that many prize-winning photographs are accidents and that the photographer, using his or her camera like a shotgun, scattering shots here and there, should certainly come up with one acceptable exposure. I wish it were true, as it is with some photographers, that all could take assignment after assignment and consistently produce excellent photographs. Many photographers are aware of the effect of light on the scene and can, and do, translate that onto the film. But most are not that capable. Their troubles all stem from this one problem.

Since we view a scene or an object in the scene by reflected light we also view each object in the scene as a whole, not seeing each object as particles or elements of grain, color or shapes in light and dark. This use of the "Gestalt" theory is fine when trying to understand perception, but it often produces errors, since the photographer should look at each detail in the viewfinder, break it down into parts and estimate the same detail as it would appear on the processed transparency. This means that light and dark, objects near and far, and every important detail should be critically examined by parts, not by wholes.

If the subject is a portrait personality, the photographer must brush aside involvement with the personality for the moment and look instead to the parts or elements that make up the view; critically analyze these, and translate them into the finished film. Ask such questions as "Is there too much contrast?" "What is the ratio of light to dark?" "If tones are dropped out, what is the effect on the final photograph?" "Just what tones are dropped and where?" "Should the subject be lighted more flatly to counteract the effect of the dropping of tones?"

Since film types and processing both have characteristics, the photographer should use his or her knowledge of these effects and estimate the translated image to the finished film. Perhaps some study under a Large Format Food Photographer would be good training for a beginner. I remember my own apprentice training. Reciprosity and bellows draw were a way of life for so many years that now, I find it difficult to expend large amounts of film. My habits are to think before I expose and to think about many things other than exposure, depth of focus or bellows draw. The translation of the color of an object in the scene to the final transparency is the prime consideration.

The most important lesson I ever learned was that the groundglass/viewfinder image had little relation to the final photograph and that the responsibility rests with the photographer to know what is taking place as he or she exposes.

# 48 Photographers' Popular Misconceptions

1. *When you're doing product photography the client should give you the product and allow you to do your own thing.*

This is probably the worst way to photograph a product, at least for the small studio photographer. For a number of reasons it's *always* best to have the client in the studio at the time of the shooting. He or she can and should approve of any of the changes in layout that often come up during the shooting due to characteristics and limitations of lenses, lighting and depth of field. It's always best to shoot a 4 × 5 Polaroid and have him approve it. It also serves as an exposure/lighting check for you. Furthermore, the client knows what to expect. He's not surprised when he gets the transparency.

Conversely, "doing your own thing" in studio product photography can be an invitation to a "planned disaster," since you don't know what the client thinks the photograph will look like. He might very well have seen some illustrations by a famous photographer of a mundane product photographed on the Utah Salt Flats or the Arizona desert using an 8 × 10 camera with all sorts of exotic flash and much magenta filtration. He might expect that you're simulating all this in your 10 × 10-foot studio. What's in the client's mind has got to be carefully extracted.

2. *In order to light a product properly, you must place one light near the camera or 45 degrees to the right or left and have a second light for a fill on the opposite side.*

In the trade we call this "Deadsville, USA" photography. It is true that you may need a minimum of two lights, or one light and a fill, or you may need a half-dozen lights or none. The determination of what kind of lighting is a very precise approach to professional studio photography, but most good illustrations of things are lit from behind with backlighting as the "main" and a gentle fill from the front. The exposure is based on the degree of rim lighting and detail wanted, since the front or visible part of the photograph is dark or dimly visible. The documentary approach to product photography using frontal lighting is used in the cheaper catalogues and sales sheets, but rarely do these have the "pizzazz" of an illustration that's back-lit.

3. *Using colored paper background enhances the product and adds "life" to the photograph.*

Not at all; almost never. The danger in using a colored paper under and around a product is what we call "subject failure." As an example in the extreme, a red paper background under, say, a yellow product, might cause the yellow to take on some of the red color becoming orange partly due to the "subject failure" of color film. Sort of a Murphy's Law—if the majority of the area of a sheet of film is one solid color, any object in the area will take on that color by "bleeding." The effect is exacerbated by using highly diffuse lighting such as tents or umbrellas, since the lighting will reflect or bounce light from the foreground and background into the product or subject. Although this might not be too objectionable in some products, it would be disastrous where the client has trademark colors. Think of Coca-Cola red, Thermos red and IBM blue.

4. *Because of subject failure, it's best to use white as the background color.*

Not necessarily so; if the lighting is tented or an umbrella is used, the reflected white light will diffuse the color of the product. The red Thermos bottletop will photograph as pink in a tented condition. What is needed is a "sharper" light such as a straight strobe or perhaps raw quartz lighting. Under such lighting the bottle will "hold" its color, but the photograph will have unacceptable contrast and be difficult to reproduce. There's a fine line between the flatness of the tent and the raw lamp; getting just the right amount of diffuse light is the mark of the master. Of course, there are hundreds of variations and combinations of lighting between the two examples.

Only experience and good teaching can show you exactly which is best for a given set of circumstances. If you're in doubt or not quite as proficient as you'd like to be, work with an umbrella.

5. *When in doubt, use an umbrella or a tent for studio-product lighting.*

This is partially true, and the statement does fly in the face of what I've said above. I'd suggest an umbrella for the beginner but I fail to see why anyone should stay a beginner longer than one full eight-hour day of experimenting and one full day of reading. The tent has a tendency to degrade the color of the product, being almost too soft. Solids become pastels. The umbrella is not quite as severe as a tent and some of the better quality umbrellas can be controlled. Matte umbrellas, mylar reflector-type umbrellas and umbrellas with diffusers, if you'd believe, and even umbrellas with a backing to prevent light from going through and losing a stop exposure, are more than adequate. Balcar or Tekno makes the best of these. They're made for their strobe lighting. (Incidentally, I heartily endorse their strobe equipment, and I do use their umbrellas on my Lowell Quartz lights.) Umbrellas reflect in people's eyes, which I find objectionable, although this is quite common in fashion photography—just check any of the fashion magazines. However, the reflection of an umbrella in a product is not acceptable and either has to be retouched out (an expensive chore) or the reflection is broken up with strips of cardboard.

In my case, where I'm doing some liquor advertisements and point of purchase sales material, I designed my own foamcore reflector lined with Reynolds Wrap and covered with mylar tracing paper. I made these about 12 × 20 feet and when they appear in the photograph they look like highlight streaks. These cost about $5 each for materials and I had a good deal of fun designing and making them with nothing more than an Xacto knife and the materials mentioned.

6. *Buying a good (expensive) light meter will assure you or nearly perfect exposures in product photography.*

We're all searching for nirvana and the magic Black Box, but it'll never be; a meter is only as good as the person using it. After all, no meter can think, so all subjective judgments have to be made by the photographer. I do think that a reliable, repeatable meter is important. Any one of Spectra, Gossen, Minolta among others is more than satisfactory. Spot meters require being precise in reading colors as gray. The best way to use a spot meter is to cut up an 8 × 10 gray card into four 4 × 5 cards and place them in the picture area at shadow and highlight areas. Be sure to remove them before exposure. Anyone in need of some lovely 8 × 10 transparencies with little gray cards here and there?

The best way to meter for a beginner in commercial photography is to buy a good incident light meter and place it dead center of the picture area and use the resultant reading; then bracket, one each on either side. The latitude of the film will usually be wide enough to give you a good transparency.

7. *You'll never need a tricolor meter, besides you can "wing it" with filters.*

That has some truth to it. Outside you can "wing it"—an 81A will cover you for cloudy days; an 82A for morning and evening when the sky is quite yellow;

the polarizer to control reflections and to saturate the sky and darken it; a Skylight 1A for knocking out some ultraviolet rays. Yes, outdoors you might get away with a few filters. Indoors in a studio environment, you wouldn't appear to need a tricolor meter because the quartz lights are 3200K and balanced for tungsten emulsions and strobe is 5500K and balanced for daylight films. All of the above is reasonable and true, but what if the client's problems don't drop into nice little pigeon holes? The next client may ask you to photograph under fluorescent light mixed with daylight. Then he'll ask you to go down into the factory and photograph under mercury vapor light with a little bit of fluorescent and some daylight thrown in —a nice broth. For awhile there, we all thought we had it solved with the FL-B and FL-D filters; but they're simply not good enough. Lighting under the conditions mentioned is extremely tricky. Exposures and color balances can and often do become horrendous. The only solution is a tricolor meter. If you're getting this kind of assignment, start saving your pennies, on the market, the Spectra Tricolor Meter and the Minolta Color Meter. Whatever you do, don't buy one until you've tried it. Don't bother with simple situations, go directly to a mixed lighting condition and make tests. This is a new culture; only successful photographers can play in this game.

8. *Home or small studio processing of transparencies or negatives in rotary-drum processors does not yield as high a quality as sending them out to professional labs.*

This is simply not true. It is true that the big labs have sophisticated temperature and chemical replenishment controls, but that's no guarantee of high quality processing. Many labs use their chemistry beyond normal tolerances and sometimes exceed the exhaustion rates. The color balance simply cannot be monitored on a roll-by-roll basis. I would hazard a guess that almost all labs have a percentage, perhaps small, of out-of-color balance rolls returned to the customer. These labs, any lab, will cite complaint figures as being so small as to be almost insignificant. This is true because so few people complain and those who are aware of out-of-color balances blame themselves for not properly filtering. Whenever I receive Kodachrome slides back (I can't process Kodachrome) and they're out of balance, I blame the lab, but I don't complain because there are so many variables. The newer Ektachromes such as EPD and EPT are so sensitive to temperature variances that out-of-color balance could conceivably be my fault for carrying them in a warm camera case (not likely with me) or leaving the roll in the camera beyond a full day (likely with me). The so called "amateur" films, ED and ET, aren't temperature-sensitive, but I haven't found the secret to the proper filter balance yet. I've given up on them. EPY (ASA 50 tungsten) and EPR (ASA 64 daylight) are similar in characteristics to the higher-speed films but grainier. I use only the higher-speed films because then I have a choice, since so much of my photography uses tele-extenders and/or extension tubes, both of which cut effective exposure by at least two full stops. When I use both I have losses of between three and four stops so I need the higher-speed films. If I need less exposure I use neutral-density filters.

When you consider that processing at home, again in a small drum such as the Unicolor Film

Processing Drum on their reversing agitator and in Unicolor E-6, is much cheaper, easier and more likely to yield high quality (in-color balance) slides, you should begin to investigate the procedure. It is true that the same problems exist as outlined above, but by following their instructions, you almost can't miss.

When Kodak switched from 75-degree processes they threw a monkey wrench at the small professional photographer. The reason for the change was to shorten the time of processing, since "time is money." So the amateur photo-finishing market was the beneficiary. Remember, *that is* the market for photography. So many professionals think the manufacturers exist for them and that the amateurs are the poor relations. This is not true, but just another popular misconception. The professionals are the poor relations.

The problem is easy to understand. If you have liquid chemicals on your darkroom shelf, it is most likely to be at the same temperature as the darkroom —normally 75 degrees. When you proceeded to mix, you used tap water at 75 degrees and since you usually processed in the same room temperature, your chemicals remained at 75 degrees, or quite close to it. With the new temperatures, you're mixing odd amounts of liquid which are at 75 degrees from sitting on the shelf, with very hot tap water at say 120 degrees trying to reach 105 degrees. Even if you do reach your goal, the next step probably contains different amounts of "A" or "B," or whatever. You have absolutely no idea of what temperature tap water to mix with the chemicals so that the final solution is at 105 degrees (processing temperature).

Your problem doesn't end there either. While

you're mixing the third or fourth solution, the first one, sitting around at 105 degrees, has skidded down to 95 degrees, so you start playing games with hot-water jackets to bring the temperature up and while you're doing that, the others start their downward turn. Enough to make a photographer tear his hair!

The answer is either one of the newer fancy-priced automatic processing machines, the least expensive of which is over $4,000, or you could wait until a manufacturer comes out with a small plastic tub with a pump and temperature control and some method of holding the graduates in without their floating away, and fairly precise temperature control. There are some already on the market, but there seems to be something wrong with each. Unicolor is supposed to have a machine under $325 capable of holding all the mixed chemicals at 105 degrees for as long as you wish.

I'm a little luckier than most people. I have a Colenta 30H for my large sheet films, but that costs around $3900 with reels. Surprisingly, I use the Uni-drum and Unirolor for roll films, but I must admit that I dance around in that darkroom and God help me if the phone rings or someone pushes the doorbell!

I use Unicolor's chemistry because EK recommends "pre-heating" drums and tubes for six minutes and "incubation" for four minutes. Unicolor EK-Z-119 solves the pre-heating and incubation by a *pre-soak,* and I find the procedure a lot easier and much quicker both in the preparation of the chemistry and the processing time.

I've often had the professionals who visit me say, "But isn't Unicolor chemistry, amateur chemistry?" I usually tell them that if you whisper when you're processing, the professional film won't know it's being processed in amateur chemistry. That may be unfair of me, but this remark on their part is annoying to me. The inference is that the chemistry is inferior somehow, or perhaps because EK didn't manufacture it, it won't work as well or yield as good results. This is simply not true, although as a stockholder I appreciate the effectiveness of EK advertising. You would be quite surprised to know that many major laboratories processing thousands of rolls of EK daily use other than EK chemistry. Hunt is easily one of the biggest. (Of course, this does not apply to Kodachrome processing.)

Don't be frightened or intimidated by processing. It is easier, quicker, less expensive, and you usually have a better color balance when you process your own film.

9. *Since you're a professional, you should read the professional magazines but not necessarily read the "amateur" magazines.*

This is a double-barreled one. First, I feel any serious professional should read as many magazines devoted to photography as he can, whether they are professional or amateur. Besides reading those related to photography, he should read voraciously everything he can in the arts and current events. In tracing some of my best photographic sales and assignments back to their origins, I discover that many were stimulated by something I read that was not necessarily connected with photography.

I issue a warning about reading professional magazines, though. I find that many tend to perpetuate old-fashioned photographic ideas, styles and customs and not modernize their approach to new styles in photography even though they do herald new equipment. This dogmatic philosophy, if accepted as "Holy Writ," is really a placebo to photographers who don't want to change, who feel secure in the belief that this is the way photography should be done, and so be it. The myopic view or tunnel vision tends to limit any artistic view and is financially disasterous to the professional.

On the other hand, the so-called "amateur" magazines are constantly bombarding the visual senses with innovative, provocative and sometimes bizarre photographic articles and essays. I find them stimulating and informative. I also sense that with the erosion of income caused by more and more "amateurs" doing their own personal photographs and more and more businesses setting up in-house photographic departments, these new ideas may very well be the photographic business of the future.

It is well known that the amateur has the time, money and equipment to make some rather superlative photographs. I don't know about their saleability, but I do know the quality exceeds most professionals' work.

In summing up, I see little reason to compartmentalize photographers strictly into amateur or professional; both have a fascinating love affair with our craft. Some simply have found a way to do it full-time knowing well they could probably make more money at something else. Conversely, I suggest that the amateur be a subscriber to the professional magazines, for in gaining more skill, the amateur can share one of the things the professional must earn—pride of achievement.

# Epilogue: Some Thoughts on the Future

I' ve never been a pessimist—oh, I've had my moments of depression, but I consider those the normal fears of any concerned person. When I write, and especially for these chapters, I try to present a positive attitude, full of good humor and with the zest for life that I really feel. But lately I've been alarmed somewhat by some questions relating to the future of our profession. I read copiously and from quite a disparate group of magazines and books. I do this with periodicals both in and out of photography to give me an advantage in knowledge that I might pass on to my readers. I take the responsibility seriously; I really try to present factual comments that might be helpful to others. This may be taken as arrogance by some—if so, I hope they're wrong.

In passing on some of my thoughts I recognize that some readers will be overly alarmed, others will dismiss what they read as pure conjecture, which is, of course, really what it is, and still others will become annoyed to the point of being upset—and at me, since rarely do humans blame themselves. Let me enumerate some of the problems I feel photographers must face in the coming years:

First is the energy crisis. This will not necessarily affect us as we might think. I see a shortage of water as just as important as any shortage of gasoline and heating oil.

Next I am concerned at the lassitude of the economy—we really haven't fully recovered from the downturn of 1973–1974, and the malaise continues.

I'm disturbed at the inability of the government to stem the rising tide of inflation. Prices and wages are spiraling ever higher, even to the point where shaky businesses will certainly perish.

And again at the national level—the general moral malaise. When in history has our national moral position been so low? International graft, bribery of public officials, payoffs by our largest and most prestigious corporations—what has happened to the concepts of honesty, integrity, responsibility and moral forthrightness?

Religion is a farce—the church is no longer the leader in the molding of our ethics. No longer are we looking to the church and synagogue for moral strength.

And the family—where is the strong, well-knit family unit, supportive of each member, where the integrity of one becomes the integrity of all?

What about photographic problems? First off, photography is a luxury, no matter how you rationalize or justify its existence. In a condition of dire need, only the well-to-do will be buying. True, photography has turned the corner from being a fad, a toy, a hobby and is now so ingrained in industry and our culture as to insure a permanent place for itself as a necessary craft.

What about photographic equipment and supplies? New equipment has some rather astonishing price tags. Some of the new cameras cost in the thousands; processing machines are offered to the small studio photographer at prices that represent his or her entire investment just a few short years ago. Even photographic color paper and chemical kits are so expensive as to make mistakes financially disasterous. Cameras are presented on the market and are totally obsolete within minutes of the purchase. A few notable exceptions are Hasselblad, Olympus, Canon and in the larger formats, Cambo, Linhof and Sinar. But have you priced any of these? At least ten years ago, I warned that we were purchasing systems, not cameras. To maintain your competitive position you must have a formidable investment in a system.

Now that I've enumerated some of our problems, do I have some thoughts on how to solve them? I do. I mean no presumption in what I say when I suggest that our first task is to set our personal house in order. I am a firm believer in that a person with good character will persevere over one of moral laxity.

As to the energy crisis, I'm convinced we're in for rationing at the least and perhaps even worse. The

President gives us fair warning—Congress hears not well. Gas is no longer an abundantly available fuel at the millions of stations around the country. Two dollars a gallon is no longer an unreasonable price to expect to have to pay. Water is already in short supply in some sections of the country and will continue to be for some time. Water is endemic to photography, and until dry processing is accomplished as it is with, say, Polaroid, we must expect some form of curtailment—at the very least, price penalties.

Anyone who contemplates purchasing new equipment had better spend some time studying the future technological advances as they pertain to photographic apparatus. For instance, in enlargers the new Vivitar VI with a fibre-optic light source, dichroic filtration and condensers all in one enlarger, is light years ahead. Similar advances are missing in strobescopic lighting units. Meters are just now getting into the act, with Minolta leading the field with the Auto-spot 1 degree; the Autometer; their foot candle meter and, of course, their three-color meter. Photo Research has a new family of meters that are all excellent but the best is still their Tricolor meter and the Combi Professional II. Gossen excels in their famous new Luna-Pro SBC and the Panalux can't be beaten as a foot-candle meter. Anyone who buys a camera or meter with a CDS cell is just not knowledgeable.

The new professional Ektachromes E-6 are superb films with finer grain and better shadow detail, but are hard to process because technology hasn't kept up with the advances in film. We have few small processors for 100-degree chemistry. A small company, Unicolor, is right on top of most of the film advances with superb chemistry, easy to use and still my favorite.

We have to find ways to process without water. For black and white, we need new advances in stabilization techniques and in color I'm pinning my hopes on Polaroid as mentioned in previous chapters, as their dry Polacolor enlargements are the prints of the future.

Photographers are still provincial, still concerned essentially with their locality. They must branch out to service the world if necessary. I don't know what I'd do if I didn't have clients in Japan, Denmark, Germany and England, as well as many around the United States. Most of these clients have never seen me or my studio, nor do they care to— since they buy images.

As to the economy, I am as confused as the next person. I hesitate to save since the interest in banks is less than the inflation rate. Stocks and bonds are still a form of gambling. I've always preached to invest in yourself. For me, this is my way. My own museum-mounted prints are my hedge against inflation and represent my retirement policy income.

Dilettantism is the death knell of professional photography. There was a time when one could moonlight as a professional with a small investment and gradually build a business. Today, to practice professionally, one must constantly study to upgrade his or her professionalism. Mediocrity is a thing of the past—at least with the bigger accounts.

Just as cameras and other photographic apparatus have improved in technology—and this has benefited the professional—so has this same benefit been passed on to the amateur. He, in turn, no longer needs a professional for a smashingly good color photograph of his family or even his business. In most cases, he'd rather make the photographs himself. And, it's a rare corporation today that has to call an outside photographer—most have quite sophisticated departments quite capable of performing the ordinary tasks in photography.

Maybe that's it, maybe we need to be even more professional and more capable. Photographically, that's true, but in business acumen it's more than true—it's critical. I have a great deal of experience as a photographer and I consider myself quite savvy in this business, but I, too, fall prey to the glitter of pretty baubles such as cameras and lenses, most of them quite unnecessary to the performance of my daily photographic tasks. And I can rationalize and justify with the best. How often has a photographer shown me $10,000 worth of pretty machinery and then talked me blind on how necessary such a thing is for his business? Sooner or later this compulsive impulse purchasing is going to catch up with most of us.

So, we need to improve our own character, our relations with our fellow humans; improve our ability to perform; conserve our energy within our lifestyle; operate our photographic businesses with more professional vigor and maybe, just maybe, we'll get through this critical time.